UNCOVERING
the TREASURES
of the APOCALYPSE

UNCOVERING *the* TREASURES *of the* APOCALYPSE

Keys to Unlocking the Mysteries of the Book of Revelation

David L. Mathewson

CASCADE *Books* • Eugene, Oregon

UNCOVERING THE TREASURES OF THE APOCALYPSE
Keys to Unlocking the Mysteries of the Book of Revelation

Cascade Books
An Imprint of Wipf and Stock Publishers
199 W. 8th Ave., Suite 3
Eugene, OR 97401

www.wipfandstock.com

PAPERBACK ISBN: 978-1-7252-9221-5
HARDCOVER ISBN: 978-1-7252-9222-2
EBOOK ISBN: 978-1-7252-9223-9

Cataloguing-in-Publication data:

Names: Mathewson, David L., author.

Title: Uncovering the treasures of the apocalypse : keys to unlocking the mysteries of the book of Revelation / by David L. Mathewson.

Description: Eugene, OR: Cascade Books, 2022 | Includes bibliographical references and index.

Identifiers: ISBN 978-1-7252-9221-5 (paperback) | ISBN 978-1-7252-9222-2 (hardcover) | ISBN 978-1-7252-9223-9 (ebook)

Subjects: LCSH: Bible. N.T. Revelation—Criticism, interpretation, etc. | Bible. N.T. Revelation—Theology.

Classification: BS2825.52 M38 2022 (paperback) | BS2825.52 M38 (ebook)

VERSION NUMBER 071322

CONTENTS

ACKNOWLEDGMENTS

THE LAST BOOK OF the Bible continues to fascinate and challenge me. Most of my writing throughout my academic career has focused on Revelation, and although I am sometimes tempted to move on to focus on other books in the New Testament, the book of Revelation won't let me go and keeps drawing me back. This present book is meant to address a number of principles that should guide readers in reading and interpreting the book of Revelation. It is written primarily for a general audience, for those who have had little or no exposure to the book of Revelation, but will hopefully also prove useful to those who have a prior knowledge of the book, and even those who preach and teach it. I would like to thank Michael Thomson of Wipf and Stock Publishers for suggesting that I write this book and for encouraging me to move forward with the proposal. There are a number of people who were involved in the process of seeing this book to completion in some manner. The principles of this book were "tested" out at Colorado Community Church in Aurora, Colorado. I would like to thank Richard Powell, pastor of Spiritual Formation, for inviting me to teach Revelation to them. They attentively listened to my ideas and interacted with them in a constructive and encouraging way. I would also like to express my thanks to Caleb and Kara Mathewson for reading through part of this manuscript and offering some helpful suggestions for making it a better book. I am also indebted to Jennifer Fitzgerald for reading through the manuscript and making many suggestions for improvement and causing me to rethink many points. She was a constant source of encouragement throughout the entire writing process. My hope is that this book will serve the church by taking the fear out of reading the last book of the Bible and enabling readers to hear "what the Spirit is saying to the churches." Finally, this book was written for my grandchildren, Bentley, Greyson, and Reagan. They are a constant reminder of the more important things in life. My prayer is that they grow up to know the hope found in the book of Revelation that comes through a relationship with the Lamb, Jesus Christ!

INTRODUCTION
Revelation—A Locked up Treasure?

THE BOOK OF REVELATION has been a source of fascination and frustration for the church ever since it was first written down by a prophet named John about two thousand years ago. Though it presents itself as a "revelation" from Jesus Christ to his people (1:1), for many readers the content of the book still remains concealed or obscure. The book of Revelation claims to be an unsealed book (6; 10; 22:10), yet for many readers today the book of Revelation is still sealed up tight from them with "seven seals." Its meaning remains hidden from the reader today. There are so many competing theories of interpreting it,[1] and it contains so many strange and bizarre images: a hybrid creature of insect, animal, and human body parts, seven-headed beasts and dragons, a woman riding on an eagle, hail mixed with fire—how can I hope to make any sense of it? I have little chance of figuring out such an odd book. We usually, then, leave the book of Revelation for the expert scholar to decipher, or perhaps we simply trust our favorite preacher or authority on the book. Worse still, we may ignore Revelation altogether with a passing "it will all pan out in the end" and retreat to the safer or more familiar ground of the stories of Jesus in the Gospels, or of Paul's letters.

To use another metaphor, for many students of the Bible today, Revelation's message is *locked up* and inaccessible to the modern-day reader. When I was a young boy there was an old safe in the basement of our house that had been left there by a previous owner. I spent countless hours down in that basement trying to get into that safe with my ear up against the door, turning the dial, listening intently for the sound of "clicks," and hoping I would discover the correct combination that could finally open it. I was convinced that there were treasures to be found in that old safe. However, I never got it opened. I never figured out the right combination to get in. For

---

1. Wainwright, *Mysterious Apocalypse.*

1

most readers, Revelation is like a safe or a treasure chest with locks on it. We know that there is something valuable in it if we could just look inside; but we don't have the right combination or the keys to open it up and uncover its treasures.

However, the book of Revelation is just that, a "revelation" from God to his people (1:1). It is meant to reveal, not hide, God's truth. It is a book that promises a blessing to those who obey what is written in it (1:3). This means the entire book, not just chapters 2 to 3. As the word of God to his people that is meant to be read and obeyed, it is not an option to ignore it, or to hope that someone else has figured it all out. We need a strategy for reading this unique book. We need a set of keys that fit this last book of the Bible and will unlock its meaning.

This book you are holding is not meant to be a commentary on the book of Revelation. There are already a lot of good ones at both an academic and more popular level. It is also not meant to be a reading guide or companion to Revelation.[2] Instead, it is meant to be more of a "how to" book, a book that focuses on how to read and interpret Revelation in light of the kind of literature it is and the historical background from which it was produced. It is a "hermeneutics" (the science of interpretation), if you will, for the book of Revelation.[3] Admittedly, most misunderstandings of the book of Revelation, whether inappropriate infatuation with the book that speculates how it is being fulfilled in our own day, or fear that causes us to ignore the book, stem from a failure to understand what kind of book Revelation is and the appropriate principles for reading it. However, an understanding of the interpretive keys to understanding Revelation can help us unlock the treasures of this otherwise enigmatic book. Understanding the appropriate interpretive keys will not solve all the problems of interpreting Revelation, nor guarantee that we will all agree on the book's meaning. But it will get us off on the right foot and keep us from inappropriate and fanciful interpretations. The following chapters will explore the most important keys to interpreting Revelation and unlocking its treasures in light of the kind of book it is, its historical background, and the purpose for which it was written.

This book will propose and explore five important interpretive keys for unlocking the treasures of the last book of the Bible. It is interesting that when it comes to any other book of the Bible, most readers recognize the importance of asking questions such as, What kind of literature am I reading (narrative, poetry, letter)? Who was the author and who were the readers? What historical circumstances does this book address? What situation or

2. See Mathewson, *Companion to the Book of Revelation.*

3. See Klein et al., *Biblical Interpretation.*

problem(s) did the readers face? How does the context of each passage help me better understand the book? But when it comes to the book of Revelation these questions are usually ignored. The following interpretive "keys" arise from those sorts of questions: What kind of book are we reading? Who was the author, and who were the readers? What historical circumstances gave rise to the book? What is the message of the book to its first readers, and to its readers today?

Interpretive key number one is "A Genre Like No Other: What Kind of Weird Book Is This Anyway?" It explores the unique kind of literature Revelation is and how that should affect the way we read the book. Interpretation of any piece of literature depends partly on what kind of literary genre it is, and Revelation is no different. Many misinterpretations and misapplications could be avoided by understanding the unique type of literature Revelation is. Interpretive key number two is "The Mysterious World of the Book of Revelation: Did Anything Really Happen?" This chapter argues that we need to understand Revelation as a response to a specific problem or set of problems in the early, first-century church. It was not predicting some far-off time in the twenty-first century, but was addressing the needs of seven specific historical churches in the first century (see Rev 2–3). Most readers of Revelation approach the book with the assumption that John and his readers had no clue what they were seeing/reading. However, the fact that the book addressed to seven historical churches in the first century setting in Asia Minor (modern-day Turkey) suggests that we must read it in its historical context as a message to these churches and their unique needs. The third key is "God's Secret Aims in the Book of Revelation: What Was John up to?" Revelation is often seen as a book that simply predicts the future, like looking into a crystal ball or having one's fortune told. However, we need to think more clearly about what John's purpose was in writing this unique book in light of the problems in the first century church that it addressed. What was Revelation's message to the early churches? The fourth key is "An Enigma, Wrapped in a Mystery, Wrapped in a Riddle: What's This Story All about?" Revelation is not just a patchwork of predictions and prophecies, or a collection or weird images; it tells a story, it communicates a message, and the discerning reader needs to have a grasp of the story that John tells in the book. Lastly, the final key is "Beast and Bowls, Beacons, and Beelzebub: Mapping Metaphors in Revelation?" Probably the biggest issue in understanding Revelation is how to deal with the proliferation of images, or metaphors, in the book: seven-headed, fire-spewing dragons, hybrid animal and human creatures, hail mixed with fire. Many of these seem rather bizarre to us today. The tendency is then to try to make sense of them as referring to twenty-first-century realities. However, we need to start by asking what these images and symbols meant to John and his readers, and what sense they would have made within the context of Revelation.

The rest of this book will explore each of these interpretive keys for understanding the book of Revelation. Hopefully, with these keys the reader will be better equipped to unlock the treasures of this marvelous book. Each chapter will proceed to explore one of the above interpretive keys to this ancient book full of treasures and will provide examples of how each key helps to unlock the ancient text. Each chapter will end with a "Putting It into Practice" section which explores and illustrates how that principle actually works in reading this challenging book. So what keys do we need to have in our grasp as we read this book?

Key #1

A GENRE LIKE NO OTHER

What Kind of Weird Book is This Anyway?

WHAT IS THIS THING CALLED "GENRE"?

IN READING ANY PIECE of literature, we make decisions about what kind of literature we are reading. This is important because it influences the way we understand a given piece of communication, and what we expect to find in it. The term for this is "genre." *Genre* refers to the *type* or *kind* of literature to which a written (or spoken) piece of communication belongs. For example, notice the following:

To Pick Up

Bananas

Salad

Hamburger

Ketchup

Bread

Milk

Eggs

Given the structure (a list, with no full sentences) and content (food items) of this written sample, we recognize it as a grocery list. Its function is to remind us what to get when we stop at the grocery store on the way home from work. Or when we pick up a copy of the morning newspaper, or check our newsfeed online, we are confronted with different "genres": front page headlines, sports, advertisements, weather forecast, comics, political commentary. Each of these constitutes a different genre, and we don't read them in the exact same way. Each has its own design, purpose, and way of communicating. We don't expect the same thing from a comic as we do from the front page headlines, or from an advertisement or weather forecast. We read them in different ways according to their unique genre. We expect different things from different genres. For example, we don't expect cartoons to give us historical facts. They serve to entertain us or make us laugh. To use another illustration, different sporting events have their own rules that must be followed for how the game is to be played: you don't play and score golf in the same way as a game of baseball or basketball. For example, in golf a lower score is better! Baseball is structured by playing innings, golf by playing holes, and basketball by time. This applies to different kinds of literature. Each genre assumes specific "rules" for the writer to follow in writing, and for the reader to follow in reading and interpreting.

The same is true of the New Testament (and the Old Testament); it contains books of differing literary genres. In it we encounter narrative (Gospels and Acts), epistles, and smaller genres within books such as poetry or parables.[1] Each has a different structure, a different purpose, and different mode of communication. Each has different rules for reading and interpreting given the genre or type of literature they are. The literary genres that they belong to would have been common in the first century and presumably easily familiar to the first-century readers. The New Testament documents reflect the ancient literary environment of the first century. The careful reader today of the New Testament will not read the Gospels in exactly the same way as the Epistles, nor the Epistles in the same way as a parable, but will keep in mind the unique literary genres of the New Testament writings that would have been taken for granted by the ancient readers. This is especially true of the book of Revelation. The reader might be tempted to ask, "What kind of weird story is this?" It is like nothing else in the New Testament, with dragons that spew water, an elderly man with eyes blazing with fire and a sword protruding from his mouth, a lamb with seven horns and seven eyes, a swarm of locusts with animal and human-like features, a woman riding on a seven-headed beast! Though perhaps weird to us, Revelation belongs to a specific literary genre that influences how we should read the book and what we should expect to find in it. More specifically, it reflects a specific type of literature that would have been familiar to the very first readers. A failure to comprehend the unique literary type or genre of

1. For a clear and concise treatment of the literary genres in the entire Bible with discussion of principles for interpreting each genre see Fee and Stuart, *How to Read the Bible*. For more detail see Klein et al., *Biblical Interpretation*, 417–567.

Revelation lies behind most misinterpretations and misapplications of the book. And so the discerning reader will want to have a firm grasp of the kind of literature that he or she is reading when approaching this unique book. Part of the problem is that we don't really have any exact literary parallels today to what we find in Revelation. So what kind of book is this?

WHAT KIND OF GENRE IS REVELATION?

Actually, the book of Revelation consists of a combination of at least three literary genres that would have been familiar to the first readers living in the first century world. Most scholars have classified Revelation according to the three literary genres of *apocalypse, prophecy,* and *epistle.* What were these three literary types, and how do they influence our understanding of the book of Revelation? It is important to remember that we need to understand these three literary types in light of how they would have functioned and been understood in the first century when Revelation was first written and read, not according to what ideas these terms may evoke in our modern day.

Apocalypse

Most would agree that the book of Revelation can be classified as an apocalypse. When the modern-day reader hears the term "apocalypse," he/she thinks of the end of the world, World War III, a nuclear disaster, a worldwide pandemic, or some such catastrophic end to the world. Hollywood has played on apocalyptic themes in its movies, such as *Zombie Apocalypse.* But when we use the term "apocalypse" with reference to the book of Revelation, it refers to a distinctive literary type (genre), which would have been familiar to first century readers. Actually, the term apocalypse is a modern-day label that scholars have given this specific type of literature. The word "Apocalypse," translating the Greek word *apokalypsis,* literally means an uncovering or unveiling. It is found in the very first verse of the book of Revelation: "A revelation (Apocalypse) of Jesus Christ . . . " (1:1). In this verse the word is not a designation of the literary type, or genre, but a designation of what the book is about: it is an uncovering or unveiling of God's truth by Jesus Christ. However, the word "apocalypse" came to be used by scholars to refer to a type of literature that resembled Revelation in content and style. The only other book in the entire Bible that fits this literary type is the book of Daniel, although parts of Ezekiel could also be designated an apocalypse (see Ezek 1–2, 40–48) in that it records the visionary experience of a seer.

A number of other books designated by scholars as an "apocalypse," written roughly between 200 BC and AD 200, are works such as 1 Enoch, 2 Enoch, 4 Ezra, 2 Baruch, Ascension of Isaiah, and many others. These books are not found in the Old Testament or New Testament, but most were known during the time Revelation was written.

So what is an apocalypse? What do these works that are designated as apocalypses share in common? In what way does Revelation resemble this literary genre? An apocalypse is basically a type of literature that narrates the vision of a seer, unveiling divine truth about the heavenly world, the present world of the readers, and the future. The purpose of the vision is both to comfort but also exhort the hearers/listeners of an apocalypse. In addition, the apocalyptic vision was communicated in metaphors, not literally. Thus, apocalypses are filled with images of seven-headed dragons, winged creatures, fire and brimstone falling from the sky, beasts (sometimes with both animal and human features), and falling stars and planets.[2] Chapter 5 of this book will deal in more detail with interpreting John's images and metaphors. The point to note here is that a seer would receive his vision in metaphors, and then record in writing with images or metaphors that correspond to what he saw in the vision.

An apocalypse was meant to provide an alternative perspective on the world. The world is not as it appears to the eye. Apocalypses in the ancient world were often written in response to domination and oppression by foreign powers. God's people would see the world through the lenses of their situation of oppression, and through the lens of the ruling power. But an apocalypse says, "The world is not as it appears. Here is a vison that provides an alternative perspective on this world, so that you can see things in a new light and live accordingly." I remember when I got my first pair of glasses. I went home for Christmas while in college, but also needed to renew my driver's license in my home state of Montana. When I went to renew my license, I failed the vision part of the exam. I needed glasses. In a couple weeks they arrived in the mail. I thought that my vision was fine, and that I could see everything clearly. But when I put on those glasses I could not believe it! They opened up a new world for me. I could see things and details that I had not seen before. An apocalypse is like a pair of glasses or lenses. It allows the reader to see things from a whole new perspective, to see things that they had not seen before. Behind this world lies a heavenly world, and a future, that determines how this present world should be viewed. This knowledge can only come through a divine revelation, an unveiling. An apocalypse lifts the veil so that the reader/hearer can see the true reality. It

2. Mathewson, *Companion to the Book of Revelation*, 31–33.

is similar to watching a play. The person sitting in the seats only sees what takes place on the stage. But behind the curtain is the director, the stage manager, the prop artists, the costume designers, etc., all the things behind the scenes that make the play work. But it is hidden from the eye of the observer. An apocalypse lifts the curtain, so to speak, so that the reader can see behind the scenes of history and what is going on in the world to the ultimate reality that lies behind it. Behind this world lies a heavenly world, where God is seated on his throne, and beyond it is the future world towards which history is headed under God's sovereign guidance. Angels, both good and bad, play a key role in an apocalypse. Behind the earthly rulers is Satan and his demonic army. But it is not the rulers of this world who are ultimately in control; in heaven God is seated on his throne as the ruler of the universe, and behind the powers of this world lie the forces of good and evil.

This means that the main purpose of an apocalypse is not to predict the future, but to unveil and communicate through a vision the true nature of the world and reality so that the readers can see their world with fresh eyes and live accordingly. However, an apocalypse usually does look for the resolution of the earthly situation with God's intervention into history in the future, at the end of time. Then God will intervene to judge evil and to reward is faithful people. Usually, an apocalypse like Revelation is thought to provide comfort to God's persecuted people. However, apocalypses can also exhort and warn those who are compromising with the dominant powers of the day. The alternative perspective that the apocalypses provide should shape the view of the readers so that they live in an appropriate manner in the world.

Revelation, then, reflects many of these features of an apocalypse. It presents itself as a record of a vision (note the repeated use of the phrase "I saw" throughout the book) that the seer, John, had. Its designation as an "apocalypse" in 1:1 places it in a category of writings that communicate a divine revelation in the form of a vision. The repeated phrase "[I was] in the Spirit" in 1:10; 4:2; 17:3; 21:10 not only punctuates four main sections of John's vision, but marks his work out as a narrative of his visionary experience, where he was in the Spirit, probably suggesting the role that the Holy Spirit plays in the communication of the vision to John, and connecting John's visionary experience with that of the Old Testament prophet Ezekiel (Ezek 2:2; 3:12, 14, 24; 11:1, 24; 37:1; 43:5). In 4:1–2 John sees an open door into heaven and is transported there in order to experience a vision of the heavenly realms:

> After these things I saw and behold, there was an open door
> in heaven, and the first voice which I heard as a trumpet was

speaking with me saying, "Come up here, and I will show you
what is necessary to come about after these things." Immediately
I was in the Spirit, and behold a throne was set in heaven and
upon the throne was One seated.

This vision of heaven in ch. 4 is similar to what one finds in other prophetic (Isa 6:1–6) and apocalyptic texts (Ezek 1–2). Like other apocalypses,
John is privileged to be given a glimpse into the heavenly throne room. Like
other apocalypses, angels also play a role in Revelation, mediating the vision
to John in key instances (17:1; 21:9). All of this gives an "other worldly" air
to John's vision. Moreover, Revelation communicates in the form of symbols
and metaphors, not literally. In reading Revelation, one enters the world of
dragons, beasts, human and animal hybrid creatures, a scroll that is eaten,
bowls full of plagues, figures covered with eyes, etc. Revelation refers to real
persons, places, and events, in the present day of the readers and in the
future. But it describes them not with literal or scientific language, but with
the language of metaphor, the preferred mode of communication in apocalyptic works. Chapter 5 below will be devoted to exploring the metaphorical
language of Revelation and how to interpret it. All that one needs to know
at this point is that as an apocalypse, Revelation communicates in the form
of metaphor, not literally.

As an apocalypse, Revelation provides its readers with a divine perspective on the world. John's vision provides him and his readers with a
different perspective on their world. They are to see their concrete world
in light of the world that Revelation portrays through its metaphors and
images. Revelation lifts the veil as it were so that the readers can see behind
the scenes of their situation to recognize what is really taking place in their
own day.[3] Even the presence of angels in John's vision to mediate the vision
to John (17:1; 21:9), or to bring about judgment upon the earth (8:6; 15:1),
or to proclaim important messages (10:5–7; 14:6–11) gives Revelation an
apocalyptic or "otherworldly" feel and perspective, where supernatural beings are involved in the events of the world. This uncovering of the true
nature of reality can only come through a divine revelation, given to John by
God through Jesus Christ (1:1). John and the first readers of Revelation find
themselves in a world dominated by the Roman Empire, and their godless,
oppressive regime. The next chapter of this book (ch. 2) will be devoted to
the historical world of the book of Revelation and the events that lie behind
it, and how this helps us make better sense of the book. Revelation allows
the readers to see their world through a different lens, through the lens of
John's vision and the images and metaphors with which John communicates

---

3. Bauckham, *Theology of Revelation*, 7.

his vision. It creates a visionary world, though a real one, that the readers can enter that will help transform their perspective on their first century Roman-dominated world in order to shed fresh light on their situation. Armed with this new perspective the readers can respond in an appropriate manner and live in the world in conformity with God's perspective on what is going on.

Though Revelation's main concern is not with eschatology, or end-time events, it does envision the wrap-up of history with the intervention of God with the coming of Christ at the end of history to bring final judgment and salvation, and to renew all things (Rev 19–22). However, Revelation is just as concerned with the present time of the first readers and helping them make sense of their unique situation. When it does refer to end-time events in the final chapters, it is still to help the readers make sense of their situation by placing their situation against the backdrop of God's overall purposes for the entire world in the future. The present world of the readers, under the rule of the Roman Empire, is not all there is. Beyond it lies a future world where God will bring about his purposes and recreate all things.

Perhaps the closest modern-day analogy to how Revelation communicates which some have noticed is the political cartoon. A political cartoon refers to real events in the political landscape, but it depicts them with images and metaphors, not literally. The images used are often exaggerated in order to enforce a point, and so that the reader reacts in a certain way. Some of the imagery is stereotypical, that most readers are familiar with (for United States politics, the eagle refers to the USA; a donkey or elephant refers to their two major political parties, Democrat and Republican; the figure of Uncle Sam refers to the US government). Political cartoons, like the book of Revelation, have a way of capturing the imagination and providing a specific perspective on the actual events of the day. They refer to real person and events in our political landscape, but they describe them with metaphors. The main difference is that Revelation paints its pictures through words.

However, Revelation has some key differences from other works usually considered apocalypses. First, like other New Testament books, John is convinced that the end-time kingdom predicted by Old Testament prophets has already been inaugurated by Jesus Christ. Unlike other apocalypse, John is not waiting for the end to arrive, for God to one day intervene into history. The end-time resurrection has already begun with the resurrection of Christ, bringing about death's defeat (1:18). The people of God are already a kingdom of priests (1:5–6) who witness to the reality of God's and the Lamb's rule. Satan has already been defeated (Rev 12), and the church already finds themselves in the period of tribulation and persecution (1:3; 11:2–10). These events have yet to reach their climax (Rev 19–22), but the end has already been inaugurated in the person of Jesus Christ. Second, another key difference is that most apocalypses were what are known as *pseudonymous*, that is, they were written in the name of a famous historical figure of the past (but dead at the time of the real writing of the apocalypse), addressing that famous figure's own contemporaries. The current author (whoever he/she was) and readers were to see their situation in light of the past. However, John does not cloak his writing in an ancient figure and audience long past, but writes in his own name and addressed his readers directly, Christians living in seven cities in ancient, first-century Roman Empire (1:4; 2–3). As we will see below, Revelation is also a letter, which John uses to directly address his audience and their historical situation. But there are enough similarities with works considered "apocalypses" to note Revelation's relationship to them and to adjust our interpretive lenses accordingly. At the end of this chapter we will summarize the principles for interpreting Revelation given the kind of literature that it is.

Prophecy

Revelation also belongs to the literary genre of ancient prophecy. Revelation designates itself a prophecy no less than five times in the book (1:3; 22:7, 10, 18, 19). Prophecy was not uncommon in the first-century church. We find references to prophecy in the early Christian church in other places in the New Testament, such as Acts 10–11 and 1 Cor 11; 12–14. But how would the first readers have understood prophecy in the first century? For most modern-day readers, the notion of prophecy immediately conjures up ideas of predictions of the distant future, much like a fortune teller. For many, prophesy carries the connotation of end-time prediction that have not yet reached their fulfillment. However, this would not have been an accurate depiction of prophecy for the first-century Christians. For them, prophecy was not primarily about predicting the future (though it can do that at times). Instead, it was first and foremost about proclamation of a message revealed by God to a human speaker/writer, which contains both words of comfort as well as warning and exhortation. This prophetic message was directly relevant to the present situation of the hearers/readers. It was a call to the people to respond in obedience and faithfulness, not to satisfy their curiosity by predicting some far-off time and place.

Scholars often like to distinguish between the functions of *foretelling* and *forthtelling* in prophecy.[4] The former, foretelling, has to do with predicting the future. Prophecy can do this, but often the prophets predicted the

4. Klein et al., *Biblical Interpretation*, 462.

near future of the readers, not necessarily some time period centuries or millennia down the road. But most scholars are in agreement that prophecy is more interested in and concerned with the second function, *forthtelling*. Forthtelling concerns the communication of God's message to the present time of the readers, a message that is directly relevant to them and their circumstances. The prophetic message was a call to obedience, and included announcements of divine judgment or salvation.

Revelation clearly belongs to the literary genre of prophecy. As we have already noted, five times John refers to his work as a prophecy, and his activity is designated as "prophecy" in 10:11. Furthermore, John undergoes what resembles a prophetic commission (1:9–21; 10), much like the prophets of old, such as in Isa 6 or Jer 1. His work contains calls to repentance and exhortations to obedience, especially in the messages to the seven churches in chapters 2 and 3. The seven "letters" to the churches in Rev 2–3 are actually seven prophetic proclamations communicated by Jesus through his messenger John to the church, exhorting them to repentance and faithfulness.

Unlike the prophecies Paul addresses in 1 Cor 12–14, which seemed to be direct utterances given to the church, the prophecy of Revelation is in the form of an apocalyptic vision, so it could be labeled an *apocalyptic prophecy*. As a prophet John is primarily interested in *forthtelling*, that is, proclaiming a message for his readers in his own day. It is a message that warns of judgment, but also promises salvation to those who are faithful. However, as a prophecy it does contain *foretelling*, future prediction, where John does anticipate the final wrap-up of history with the second coming of Christ to bring end-time judgment and salvation and to inaugurate a new creation (see Rev 19–22). But even the visions of the end in Revelation are not meant to satisfy the curiosity of the readers, or to speculate as to exactly what will happen and in what order, but to assure the readers that God is going to bring history to its intended goal, and that God's redemptive purposes will prevail and be accomplished. This should inspire hope in the people of God and encourage them to remain faithful and obedient in the present.

As a prophet, John makes clear that his work actually stands in line with not just the Christian prophets of his day, but the Old Testament prophets, such as Isaiah, Ezekiel, and Jeremiah, and Daniel. John draws on their language and imagery, and even their experience, to communicate his own prophetic message to his readers. His messages of judgment and salvation reflect common prophetic themes. John writes at the climax of the Old Testament prophetic tradition, gathering up their prophecies and showing how they find their fulfillment.[5] However, what distinguishes John

5. Bauckham, *Theology of Revelation*, 5.

from his Old Testament predecessors is that he writes in light of how these prophecies find their fulfillment in Christ, now and in the future. As we have already seen, like other New Testament writers John sees the promises of the Old Testament fulfilled already in the first coming of Christ, in his death and resurrection, even though still awaiting their final consummation and fuller fulfillment at the second coming of Christ at the end of history. Therefore, at the end of his book John actually reverses the strategy of Dan 12:4, 9, where Daniel is told to seal up the words of his book, because they are for a future time. To seal up a work was to hide its contents for a distant future time. When you send a letter in the mail today you seal the envelope. Only when it is unsealed by the recipient can its contents be read. But John is told just the opposite of Daniel: he is not to seal up the words of his prophecy, because "the time is near" (Rev 22:10). John is not addressing events in the distant future, but sees those events predicted in the Old Testament as already being fulfilled in his day, since Christ has inaugurated their fulfillment. In this way Revelation is different from other ancient apocalypses that looked to the intervention of God at the end of history for its resolution. Yet like the Old Testament prophets and apocalyptic writers before him, John still looks to the end of history for the final fulfillment and ultimate resolution of God's redemptive purposes for his people and creation. But for John the end-time events have already begun in the death and resurrection of Christ, and simply wait their final culmination.

Therefore, as a Christian prophet who stands in the line of the great Old Testament prophets of the past, John shows how their prophecies are now being fulfilled in his own day in light of how they have reached their climax in Christ. As a prophet he delivers a message from God to the people that warns them of judgment for unfaithfulness, but encourages them to remain faithful and obedient in light of the salvation God has already accomplished in Christ and will bring to its climactic fulfillment in the future. As a prophecy, Revelation is not meant to provide information to speculate about the future or construct a detailed chart and timeline of end-time events. Rather, the main burden of prophecy is to exhort and call forth obedience from the people of God.

Epistle

In addition to being an apocalypse and a prophecy, Revelation also shares features of a first-century epistle or letter. That Revelation is also a letter usually gets overshadowed by our focus on the apocalyptic and prophetic elements of John's work. The careful reader of the New Testament is already familiar with numerous letters written by Peter, James, John, and especially the apostle Paul. An epistle was a common literary form used in the first century by early Christian leaders to address their readers (churches). Most anything could be communicated by a letter back then. Today, we still send letters, but more normally address people with emails or other electronic forms to communicate information, ask for a favor, or just maintain contact. Usually, a typical first-century letter as found in the New Testament contained at least an introduction, where the author identified himself and his readers along with a greeting ("X to Y, greetings"), the main body of the letter, and a letter closing. A letter in the first century allowed the author to address a specific audience who had specific needs or problems. New Testament scholars refer to first-century letters as *occasional*. That is, the letters were brought about by a specific occasion; they addressed specific problems or issues facing the early church. The apostles did not just sit down and compose letters to be included in the Bible. Therefore, when the church in Galatia faced the problem of Judaizers insisting the Gentile Christians submit to circumcision and the Old Testament law, Paul instructed them with a letter. When the church was facing false teachers that promoted immoral living by calling into question whether God would intervene in judgment, Peter wrote a letter to call them to holiness and convince them that Christ will indeed return in judgment (2 Peter). When scattered Jewish Christians required instruction on living out their faith wisely in the world in the face of a number of circumstances, James wrote them a practical letter. Letters, then, could be used by early church leaders to address directly the specific issues, crises, and needs of their specific audience. To understand these New Testament letters correctly one must have a grasp of the readers and the problem or issues being addressed. Presumably, these letters communicated information that would have been relevant to the needs of these audiences and therefore understood by them.

John clearly intends the book of Revelation to be a letter. He couches his apocalyptic prophecy in the form of a letter. His work begins like an epistle, with a typical introduction that identifies the author and his readers and includes a greeting, and the source of the greeting: "John, to the seven churches in the province of Asia. Grace and peace to you from him who is, and who was, and who is to come, and from the seven spirits before his throne, and from Jesus Christ, the faithful witness, the firstborn from the dead, and the ruler of the kings of the earth" (1:4–5). Compare this to the introduction to one of Paul's letters: "Paul, an apostle of Jesus Christ by the will of God, to the saints in Ephesus, the faithful in Christ Jesus. Grace and peace to you from God our Father and the Lord Jesus Christ" (Eph 1:1–2). John clearly identifies the recipients of his letter as seven historical churches in first-century Asia Minor, our modern-day Turkey (1:4, 11; 2–3). Then, the book ends with a letter closing: "The grace of the Lord Jesus be with God's people. Amen" (22:21). Therefore, Revelation was actually a circular letter that would have been delivered to and circulated among the seven churches, and perhaps other churches as well. The first audiences of Revelation would have heard this letter read to them (1:3). By framing his book in the form of a letter, John is addressing his readers directly and the specific circumstances and issues that the churches face. All seven churches were in cities that were in the center of first-century Roman Empire. Each was struggling in some way to maintain their faithful witness to Christ in the context of the pagan Roman world. You can read about the issues that each of the churches faced in Rev 2–3. The next chapter of this book will explore in more detail the world of the first Christians and the challenges to their allegiance to God and Christ. By framing his entire prophetic vision in the form of a letter, John shows that his entire book (not just chs. 2–3) is just as occasional as any of Paul's letters, that is, it is meant to address the specific needs of a specific community. John wrote in response to real problems in the churches and communicates something to them that they could understand and that would address the crisis and issues they faced. Therefore, Revelation must be interpreted in light of its original historical context, and in light of what the author was trying to communicate and what the first readers would have understood.[6]

CONCLUSION: PRINCIPLES
FOR INTERPRETING REVELATION

So what does all of this mean for interpreting the book of Revelation? Interpretation of any biblical book depends partly on correctly assessing what kind of genre the book belongs to. Figuring out the exact genre does not guarantee that all the interpretive problems will vanish. But it does ensure that we will get off on the right foot in our reading of any biblical book. Just like knowing the rules of a baseball game will not guarantee that you play it well, but it will help you to play the game correctly. This is especially true of the book of Revelation. Many speculative misinterpretations of the book could have been avoided by approaching it through a correct understanding of the kind of literature that it is. Countless short books and brochures have circulated, and will continue to do so, which read Revelation as a prediction of events in our present-day world. Countless sermons have played on the fears of the people of God by predicting how close they are to the end. The

6 Fee and Stuart, *How to Read the Bible*, 253.

visions of Revelation are treated as a forecast of our modern day technological and political landscapes. Many have gone further and have attempted to
plot our existence in relationship to the end—how close are we to seeing the
second coming of Christ? In light of the correspondences between Revelation and events in our own day, surely we are living in the last generation
who will witness the return of Christ! A failure to consider the kind of book
we are dealing with when it comes to a difficult book like Revelation is to in-
vite misunderstanding. We have tried to show in this chapter that the book
of Revelation belongs to three literary genres that would have been familiar
to the first readers and should influence the way we read Revelation: apocalypse, prophecy, letter. So what principles should guide us in interpreting
any section of Revelation? What principles for interpreting the book arise
out of this unique combination of literary genres? I suggest at least the following (it is fitting that the list has seven!):

1. Focus on the original historical context.

   Revelation must first of all be understood in light of the original historical context in which it was written. Revelation was addressed to
   seven historical churches in first-century Asia Minor, living under the
   domination of Roman imperial rule. The next chapter will address in
   more detail the historical backdrop for the book of Revelation. It is
   important to recognize that Revelation was a specific response to first-
   century Christians struggling to live out their faithful witness in the
   context of their historical context and culture. We are accustomed to
   asking this question of any other book in the New Testament. Why did
   Paul write Galatians, for example? Who were his readers? What were
   their circumstances and the problems they were facing that caused
   Paul to write what he did? Who were the Judaizers and what were they
   teaching? How did Paul respond to these issues faced by the first readers? But we often ignore these questions when it comes to the book of
   Revelation. However, given the kind of book that it is, we must first
   place Revelation in its historical context, and ask how it was a response
   to the first-century Christian readers and the issues they were facing.
   Revelation was addressed to seven churches who are identified in 1:4;
   2–3. Revelation is a prophetic message to the contemporary situation
   of these first readers, and as a letter it is as occasional as any of Paul's
   letters. So a very important key for unlocking the treasures of the book
   of Revelation is to keep a close eye on the original historical context
   of the book. Any interpretation of any section of Revelation must ultimately be consistent with its historical context.

2. A valid interpretation must be what the author could have intended and the very first readers have understood.

As a corollary to the first principle is this second one: for any interpretation of Revelation to be valid it must be something that the author could have intended and the first-century readers could have grasped. Again, most speculative popular readings of Revelation that focus on how modern-day events are the fulfillment of Revelation's visions miss this principle. Instead, modern readers want to correlate Revelation's images with computers, nuclear wars, pandemics, modern methods of warfare, the Middle East, and the internet. It is as if John gazed into a crystal ball and saw the future, but did not have language to describe what he saw. So he did the best he could with his limited, first-century perspective. But now we are in a better position to understand what it was that John actually saw. Recently a well-meaning church member confidently told me that John had no idea what he was seeing and his readers had no idea what they were reading . . . but now we do! However, the literary genre of Revelation leads us in the exact opposite direction. John and his readers understood these visions, and we are the ones that have to do the hard work, as with any biblical text, to determine what John was intending to communicate and what his readers would have understood. Any interpretation that John could not have possibly intended and his first readers could not possibly have understood is probably wrong.

Two other features of the book support this. First, John pronounces a blessing on those who "keep" the words of the prophecy of his book (1:3). To keep the book is to obey it. Yet how could John expect his readers to obey a book that they did not understood or had no clue as to its meaning? The fact that John (speaking for Jesus) expects his reader to obey the book assumes that they will be able to understand it. Second, as we have seen, at the very end of the book John is told not to seal up the words of his prophecy (22:10). To seal up a book was to keeps its contents hidden for a later, future time, which is what Daniel tells his readers (Dan 8:26; 12:4). But John is told just the opposite of Daniel. It is not to be sealed up for a later time, because the time is near. The fulfillment of these events are already taking place in his readers' day; Revelation is a message directly relevant to them. Therefore, to be consistent with the kind of literature Revelation is, the careful interpreter must seek to interpret it in light of what John would have intended and his first readers, Christians living in the first-century Roman empire, would have understood.

3. Interpret Revelation symbolically, not literally.

   I have often heard and read the following adage for interpreting Revelation: "You should interpret Revelation literally unless there is really good reason not to." Due to the kind of book that Revelation is, this principle should be turned upside down: the interpreter should interpret Revelation symbolically unless there is really good reason not to. This is not an arbitrary move to symbolize Revelation because we feel like it, or because we don't know what else to do with it. This is what the kind of literature demands. Revelation is an apocalypse, and one of the key features of an apocalypse as a literary genre is that it communicates through the mode of symbols or metaphors. Revelation does refer to literal persons, places, and events. But it describes them through images and metaphors, not literally, much in the same way that a political cartoon describes real political persons and events, but through metaphors. These symbols and metaphors would have been ones that John and his readers were familiar with. Most of them came straight out of the Old Testament. Some of them would have been familiar from other apocalyptic literature, and some would have been familiar from the Greco-Roman world. The point is the images were drawn from the readers' background and experience. And John describes his visions with images that closely correspond to what he actually saw. So important is the imagery and metaphorical language of Revelation that an entire chapter of this book is devoted to interpreting Revelation's symbolism (see ch. 5).

4. Focus on the theological meaning of John's visions; don't get bogged down in details.

   With a book like Revelation, with its strange visions and images, it is easy to get bogged down in the details of the vision. We want to figure out what every detail means, what it refers to, and how precisely it will be fulfilled. Revelation becomes a code that we need to crack, so that every detail is accounted for. However, it is more important to focus on the overall meaning of the vision and its imagery, rather than obsess over every detail and trying to find a specific fulfillment. Often, the details simply reinforce the overall picture or message, and do not add specific events that must find a fulfillment. In this way, John's visions are similar to Jesus's parables. Sometimes the details in Jesus's parables simply function to add "color" to the parable and make the story work, rather than adding details that must be deciphered and given a spiritual meaning. In the parable of the prodigal son (Luke

15:11–32), the father, younger son, and older son all have a spiritual meaning, in that they refer to spiritual realities related to the kingdom of God. The father stands for God who humbles himself to accept sinners who repent, the younger son for sinners who are lost but turn to God in repentance, and the older son stands for the Pharisees, who are jealous because Jesus associates with the likes of tax collectors and sinners (see 15:1–2). However, the other details, such as the robe, the ring, the fattened calf, the servants, are not to be given an additional level of meaning; they are there just to fill out the story and make it work. The same is often true with John's visions. This means that we should focus on the overall message of the visions and not get bogged down with trying to figure out what every last detail refers to and how they will be fulfilled. For example, in the sequence of Trumpet plagues in Rev 8–9, it is far less important to figure out exactly what these judgments are or will look like, and whether they will occur in this exact sequence, than it is to note the parallel with the Exodus plagues from Exod 7–11 (see below). These trumpet judgments have way more to do with the certainty and nature of God's judgment than with exactly what they will look like. The key feature is the exodus connection. In the same way, the fact that the dragon in Rev 12:4 drags one-third of the stars from heaven down to earth may not refer to any specific event that we need to decipher, but only reinforces the picture of the power and fierceness of the dragon-Satan.

5. Expect past, present, and future references in Revelation.

Most readers of Revelation are tempted to see it as a prediction of future events. That is, Revelation only refers to events that have not yet taken place, and will only happen at the end of history right before and at the second coming of Christ. This is often tied to an understanding of prophecy that sees it as a foretelling of a future course of events, a history written in advance. However, as a prophetic letter Revelation is communicating a message that is directly relevant to its readers and helps them make sense of their own world. Furthermore, John is convinced that the time is already at hand, fulfillment is already taking place, and so his book will refer to visions being fulfilled in the time of his first readers. On the other hand, as an apocalypse Revelation is interested in how God will intervene to bring history to its intended goal in the future. And so Revelation does end with visions that have yet to find their fulfillment in chapters 19 to 22. Therefore, we should expect in Revelation a description of events that were already taking place or about to take place in the time of the first-century readers living in the Roman Empire, as well as references to the final wrap-up of history at the second coming of Christ. In chapter 6 of Revelation the seal sequence covers both the present time of the readers and the future. The first 4 seals refer to God's judgment which is already upon the Roman Empire's political and economic system. With the sixth seal we are at the Day of the Lord, the final judgment, at the end of history. There is even a reference to an event in the past in Rev 12:5. The birth of the male son is clearly a reference to the birth of Jesus Christ, an event clearly past from the standpoint of the first readers (and us today). So when we read Revelation we should expect references to the present and future time of the readers, and even the past.

6. Revelation should inspire obedience and faithfulness.

Readers usually get preoccupied with the details of Revelation's vision and trying to decipher the symbolism. But Revelation is first and foremost a call to obedience and faithful witness, not a prediction of the future or data for constructing an end-times chart. As the Old Testament prophets called on God's people to repent and return to faithfulness to their covenant with Yahweh, so John as a prophet calls his readers to obedience and faithfulness to the God they claim to worship. The entire book is bracketed with calls to obedience. In 1:3 John pronounces a blessing on those who hear the words of the book and keep it, that is, to obey it. Revelation ends likewise with a curse on those who hear it but fail to keep and obey it in 22:18–19. The image of "adding to" and "subtracting from" in these verses refer to failing to obey Revelation and diminishing its importance in the lives of the readers. The prophetic messages in chs. 2–3 contain calls to repentance, as well as encouragements to faithfulness and perseverance. Scattered throughout the book are calls for the reader to exercise wisdom and to respond appropriately, with endurance and faithfulness (12:17; 13:9, 10, 18; 14:12; 16:15). As a prophetic message to the seven churches, Revelation is a call to obedience and for the church to maintain its faithful witness in the midst of a corrupt and godless society, no matter what the consequences that brings. Any interpretation of Revelation that does not begin with or recognize this is off on the wrong foot and does an injustice to the book's main purpose.

7. Humility!

Finally, a good dose of humility is needed in order to interpret this fascinating book. Due to the complex nature of the book, the sometimes difficult and strange images, the unique type of literature, and the diverse ways Revelation has been interpreted throughout history, with this book more than any other in the Bible humility is a prerequisite when approaching it. We must realize that we do not have all the answers, and at times hold our interpretations loosely, being open to correction and change. There is no room for overly dogmatic conclusions when it comes to reading the last book of the Bible (or any other OT or NT book for that matter). The wise interpreter will cultivate the virtue of humility when interacting with Revelation!

We could add one more principle to this list, perhaps as a further reflection of our need for humility. Here if ever the interpreter needs to rely on wise teachers in the form of good commentaries (by saying 'good' commentaries, there are many that could be safely passed over!). God did not just give the book of Revelation to *me*, but to the church as the people of God. We read it in community with others. Therefore, we need to listen to wise commentators on this difficult book, in the same way we listen to experts in any other area of life; e.g., a mechanic to understand what is wrong with my car. Commentaries are our teachers, and many men and women have gone before us who have wrestled with the book of Revelation and provided their insights for us. The people of God today would be negligent if we did not listen to their guidance. There are both more academic and more popular level works that will help the diligent and curious reader, student, or pastor wrestle with this unique book. I have chosen ones which have implemented the insights discussed above and who are sensitive to the unique literary type and the historical context of the book of Revelation, while also keeping an eye on the contemporary application. The following list represents a cross-section of up-to-date commentary on the book of Revelation:

Academic

Gregory K. Beale, *Revelation*, New International Greek Testament Commentary (Grand Rapids: Eerdmans, 1999).

Craig R. Koester, *Revelation*, The Anchor Yale Bible (New Haven, CT: Yale University Press, 2014).

Mid-range

Craig S. Keener, *Revelation*, The NIV Application Commentary (Grand Rapids: Zondervan, 2000).

Ian Paul, *Revelation*, Tyndale New Testament Commentaries (Downers Grove, IL: IVP Academic, 2018).

Popular

Michael J. Gorman, *Reading Revelation Responsibly: Uncivil Worship and Witness* (Eugene, OR: Cascade, 2011).

David L. Mathewson, *A Companion to the Book of Revelation* (Eugene, OR: Cascade, 2020).

PUTTING IT INTO PRACTICE

So how do these principles actually work? How does an understanding of the literary genre of Revelation actually affect the way we read and interpret it? Let's look at a sample passage in Revelation. In Rev 13:18 the reader finds the famous number 666, the mark of the beast that people receive to enable them to buy and sell (v. 17). Here if ever one needs to apply sound principles of interpretation that arise from the kind of literature that Revelation is. This passage with the mention of the mark of the beast, 666, has been subject to much speculation. It has been identified with the internet, computer chips embedded in the hand or forehead, and other modern-day phenomena. Growing up I heard it identified as bar codes on products, and credit cards in your wallet. Several years ago I was in a restaurant and witnessed a gentleman who refused to pay his bill because it amounted to $6.66! As I write this book the world is experiencing a pandemic with the spread of COVID-19 and attempts to control it. With the emergence of a number of vaccines to curb its spread, I know a number of Christians who have identified the vaccine with the mark of the beast in 13:18. How do these interpretations of the mark of the beast, or 666, stack up with the principles outlined above? First of all, none of these interpretations would have ever been grasped by first-century readers, nor could they have been intended by John. On those grounds alone, such speculations should be rejected out of hand, or at the very least approached with extreme caution. It is imperative that one interprets the number 666 in light of the historical-cultural background of John and his first readers, and what they would have understood. Most likely, the first readers would have associated the number 666 and mark of the beast with a previous emperor, Nero. The Roman emperor Nero was one of the more volatile and evil of the emperors, who persecuted and murdered the people of God. In the world of that time, letters of the alphabet could have numerical value. It would be similar to the English language alphabet having the values of a = 1, b = 2, c = 3, d = 4, etc. In the first century one could come up with a number by adding up the numerical values of each letter in someone's name. In certain spellings of his name, Nero's name comes out to 666.[7] The number 666, which recalls Nero, reveals the true character of Rome. Nero becomes emblematic of and representative of what is at the heart of Roman rule: it is evil and means harm to God's people. In a sense John is saying, "If you want to know what the Roman Empire is really like, remember Nero!" It is as if John is saying that the spirit of Nero is still alive and well in the Roman Empire. The number 666 may also suggest falling short of the perfect number 7, or 777, pointing out the imperfect, evil character of Rome, and anything that opposes God and falls short of his character.

Furthermore, the interpreter must take seriously the apocalyptic nature of John's vision, and treat this number, or mark of the beast, metaphorically, rather than as a reference to a literal mark that people receive. The mark implies identity and belonging, and symbolizes sympathy with the Roman government and the values of the world. It is something that the people willingly and knowingly take on themselves, not something that occurs coincidentally, like $6.66 on a receipt or 666 on a credit card. In Revelation it contrasts with the mark or seal that God's people receive, which is not a literal mark but metaphorically indicates belonging and allegiance to God and the Lamb (7:3–4; 9:4; 14:1), rather than belonging to the dragon and the evil world system (the Roman Empire for first-century Christians) that he inspires.

As a prophetic warning to the churches in chapters 2 and 3, this verse is not a prediction of some future (twenty-first century) technological wonder, such as computer chips or other a physical mark or vaccine, but a warning to the churches of the dangers of collusion, even economically, with the evil world system of the Roman Empire. To take its mark is to identify with it and give it their allegiance. Revelation 13:16 calls on the church to avoid compromising their allegiance and faithfulness to God and the Lamb, and to distance themselves from belonging to and giving allegiance to a godless, oppressive, wicked empire. For a church like Laodicea that had grown wealthy and complacent by cozying up to the Roman economy, it was a wake-up call to realize what is at stake: the loss of their faithful witness.

7. Paul, *Revelation*, 240–41.

Key #2

THE MYSTERIOUS WORLD
OF THE BOOK OF REVELATION

Did anything really happen?

SEVEN-HEADED AND -HORNED BEASTS, a dragon that can spew water, locusts with human heads wearing gold crowns, eagles that can talk, hailstones mixed with fire, blood that flows as high as the bridle of a horse—this sounds more like the stuff that fantasy novels and science-fiction movies are made of, rather than a biblical book! But some see the book of Revelation just like that—it is just a fascinating account of the battle between God and evil. It does not refer to any specific events, but offers an escape from reality into a fantasy world of beasts, dragons, and slaughtered lambs. It is like watching a sci-fi movie on Netflix. It has no correspondence to the real world as we know it. Some might also see Revelation as a prediction of events that lay far off in the future. Again, it does not correspond to anything that happened in the first century, or even in our modern day. It cannot have happened yet. Rather, it predicts some future course of events that still awaits fulfillment. In either case, Revelation seems to describe a world that has little similarity with history. And if it does refer to anything in our world, whether in the first century or twenty-first century, there is no way to know what it is. So the message of Revelation remains locked up from God's people.

However, one of the important features that grows out of the kind of literary genre that Revelation belongs to (see previous chapter) is that it was written to address the needs of seven historical churches in first-century Asia Minor. It was written in a literary genre that would have been familiar to its first readers, and which would have addressed their specific situation. Revelation is a letter, addressed to the churches in cites of Ephesus, Pergamum, Thyatira, Smyrna, Sardis, Philadelphia, and Laodicea. In 1:4 John locates the book of Revelation on the map. Revelation 1:4 is the Google Maps for locating the rest of the book! It locates Revelation in a real geographical setting, and specific period in real space-time history. Therefore, like any other book in the New Testament Revelation must be understood within its first-century historical context. It must be something that addresses the needs and issues of, and therefore would have been understood by, the first readers. It was a prophetic word to them (1:3). In the same way that we need to understand what was going on in the churches in Galatia, or in Thessalonika, or in Corinth to understand why Paul wrote the book of Galatians, 1–2 Thessalonians, and 1–2 Corinthians, so it is equally necessary to understand what was going on in these seven churches in Revelation in order to understand what John, the author, was trying to communicate to those readers in the book of Revelation. As New Testament scholar David deSilva writes,

> Once we take full notice of the fact that Revelation is a letter addressed to seven very real communities of Christians spread throughout the Roman province of Asia in western Turkey, we are free to read it as a piece of communication that reveals its meaning and message most fully when we immerse ourselves in the contexts and conversations of the ancient audience.[1]

John expects his readers to understand and obey his book (1:3; 22:10). It is not for some future generation, centuries down the historical pipe from John's readers. We saw above that a key feature of apocalyptic literature is how it communicates—it communicates through symbols and metaphors. However, those symbols and metaphors refer to real people, places, and events (see ch. 5 below). As an apocalypse, Revelation is attempting to get its readers to see their world in a fresh light. Another way of saying it is that the entire book of Revelation assumes a story, the story of the first-century churches in Asia Minor whom John addresses. Much of the information about the stories of these seven church can be found in Rev 2–3 with the seven messages to the churches. We also have other information in the form of ancient writings, archeological discoveries, coins, inscriptions, etc. (you can visit the ruins of all of the seven cities today![2]) that help us to understand what was going on in the first-century world that aids us in painting a

---

1. deSilva, *Unholy Allegiances*, 11.

2. For a thorough introduction to the ancient cities in modern-day Turkey, see Mark Wilson, *Biblical Turkey*.

picture of the story behind Revelation. We need to immerse ourselves in the world and historical context of the first readers of the book. So what was going on in the seven churches in ancient first-century Asia Minor that forms the backdrop for the record of John's vision in Revelation? What issues and problems were the churches facing? Did anything really happen in the book of Revelation?

THE ROMAN CONTEXT

The book of Revelation was written during a time when Rome was the dominating world power of the day. Two well-known events from a Jewish perspective that reflected Roman power were 1) the capture of Jerusalem by the Roman army in 63 BC, ending a brief period of freedom for Israel, and 2) the destruction of the Jerusalem temple by the Roman army in AD 70. Leading up to and after this time, Rome was busy extending its empire, eventually embracing an area larger than any other previous world empire in history. The empire encompassed an area that extended to what are the modern-day countries of Britain, Spain, France, Germany, and Egypt. At the center of Roman Empire was the city of Rome, with its population around 1 million people, and the emperor who ruled over this expansive empire. More accurately, Rome was ruled by a series of Emperors, beginning with the well-known Julius Caesar (27 BC). The way that Rome kept tabs over such a large area was through dividing up the empire into *provinces*. These were regions that were under the administrative rule of Rome. One of those provinces was Asia Minor (modern-day Turkey), and all the seven cities mentioned in Rev 2–3 belonged to the Roman province of Asia Minor and were therefore directly under Roman rule. This means that whatever other cultural or religious influences were present in these cities, the dominant influence was that of imperial Rome. Virtually no one could escape its impact.

THE ROMAN EMPIRE AT A GLANCE

Since all of the churches in Asia Minor were under the thumb of Roman rule, it is necessary to understand a little bit more about the Roman Empire and its system of rule, in order to better understand how Revelation was a response to the unique situation of the seven churches. Although we are removed nearly two-thousand years from the world of Revelation, we have an abundance of knowledge of the Roman world of the first century during which time Revelation was written. First of all, Rome was a thoroughly pagan, yet religious, empire and recognized many gods (the name for this is "polytheism"). Typical cities in the Roman world, including the seven cities which John addresses in chapters 2 and 3, had temples in honor of pagan gods.[3] These cities had gods for all occasions. One of the more well-known temples was the enormous temple of Artemis in the city of Ephesus. Artemis was a very popular goddess, the daughter of Zeus, and goddess of the hunt. Another city in which John addresses a church, the city of Pergamum, was well-known for its altar to Zeus, a popular and important Greek deity.[4] These temples and altars to the Greek and Roman gods were visible reminders of the importance that the gods played in the life of the cities. They were responsible for your health, prosperity, and overall well-being. Along with temples and religious sites in honor of the pagan gods, were the temples and religious sites dedicated to Roman emperors. For example, in Pergamum there was a temple dedicated to Augustus, and the city of Ephesus had a temple in honor of the emperor Domitian (who was likely the ruling emperor when Revelation was written; see below) and his family. As a further reminder of the importance that the emperor played in the life of Rome's citizens, the heads of these emperors also appeared on coins. Reminders of Roman rule were everywhere in the form of visible images, even in your wallet!

The imperial cult—the veneration or worship of the emperor—was an important part of daily life in the Roman Empire and was particularly prevalent in Asia Minor during the time Revelation was written.[5] Worship of the emperor was encouraged through the presence of impressive temples, shrines, and altars. Most of the cities that John addressed in Rev 2–3 had temples or altars erected in honor of the emperor. All of them were influenced by the imperial cult in some way. Some of the seven cities addressed by John had priesthoods responsible for carrying out and encouraging worship of the emperor. The cities competed for a prestigious title, "Temple Guardian," which was given for building elaborate temples to the emperor. It would be a little like cities competing to host the Olympic games today, or American cities competing to host the NFL Super Bowl or MLB World Series![6] Two of the cities addressed in Rev 2–3 were granted this prestigious honor of temple guardian: Ephesus and Pergamum each won the distinction twice.[7] Life in imperial Rome would be punctuated with times of celebration, lavish occasions where hymns of acclamation would be sung to the

---

3. deSilva, *Discovering Revelation*, 45–50.

4. deSilva, *Unholy Allegiances*, 13.

5. Gorman, *Reading Revelation Responsibly*, 40.

6. deSilva, *Unholy Allegiances*, 29.

7. Paul, *Revelation*, 20; deSilva, *Unholy Allegiances*, 13.

emperor, including the ascription of titles of deity ("Lord and god"). Acts of worship towards the emperor would have been incorporated into a number of public settings, including athletic games, meals, and other occasions. Worship of the Roman emperor occurred alongside of the worship of other Greco-Roman gods, such as Zeus or the goddess Roma. Often trade and commerce were connected with worship of the Roman emperor, sometimes as a requirement for belonging to trade guilds. Unlike many countries today, such as the Unites States of America, where church and state are kept separate, with Rome politics, economics, and religion were closely intertwined. However, worship of the emperor was not imposed or enforced by the emperor himself. Enthusiasm for emperor worship came primarily at the local level, from cities like those addressed in Rev 2–3. Local officials were keen to show their loyalty and gratitude to Rome through enforcing participation in imperial worship. This would ensure that they would remain on Rome's "good side," especially if they ever needed any favors from Rome.

Second, Rome promoted a series of stories or beliefs about itself. According to the story that Rome told, Rome was chosen by the gods and was the center of the universe. This great city and empire was responsible for worldwide peace, order, prosperity, and security. A golden era had been ushered in by the Roman Empire and its emperors. Rome promoted two particular beliefs about itself: 1) "Eternal Rome." Rome was the eternal city, secure and everlasting. 2) "Peace of Rome." The Roman Empire was seen as bringing an end to conflict and war, and spreading peace and security throughout its expansive empire for all its subjects within its borders.[8] This story was enforced and recalled through the visual images of temples, altars, statues, and festivities which provided occasions to celebrate the greatness of Rome and to show honor and veneration to the emperor. The everyday citizen living within the confines of the Roman Empire could not help but be reminded every day of the debt of gratitude that they owed Rome, its emperors, and the gods for all that they experienced and enjoyed: peace and safety, order and stability, success and prosperity. Here is an ancient "public service announcement" made roughly one hundred years before John wrote Revelation. It is regarding the emperor Augustus (who ruled when Jesus was born). Imagine waking up one morning and reading this:

> Augustus, whom she filled with virtue as a benefaction to all humanity, sending to us and to those after us a savior who put an end to war and brought order to all things . . . . the birth of

8. Bauckham, *Theology of Revelation*, 36.

the god was the beginning of good news [the word in the NT translated "Gospel"] to the world through him![9]

It would be unthinkable for someone to refuse to offer the appropriate display of gratitude and honor to Rome and its emperor. This was the world that Christians had grown accustomed to. This was the world that confronted them when they woke up in the morning, left their doorstep, and walked down the street to market, or to work. Everywhere were signs of pagan and emperor worship. Everywhere were opportunities for economic prosperity. However, the Roman economy was built at the expense of many others living in the empire, and was exploitative.[10] For Christians, Rome's belief in many gods and in the emperor as deserving of worship was idolatrous and conflicted with their belief in One God. And Christians found themselves having to negotiate their Christian faith and witness in such an environment.

The discerning reader can begin to see some of the problems that living in such a world created for first-century Christians. To be involved in politics, or commerce, or many of the other every-day activities a good citizen would be involved in, would have entangled Christians in the entire system of Roman religion and beliefs, and in an economic system that was exploitative and idolatrous. Christians were being encouraged to offer worship to someone other than the true God and Jesus Christ, the Lamb. They are being encouraged to acknowledge an alternative empire to the kingdom that God had established through his Messiah, Jesus Christ. They were being encouraged to look to Rome for their salvation, peace, and security. Followers of Jesus Christ were confronted with a dilemma: to what extent can we show our allegiance to Rome and participate in imperial worship and benefit from its economy, while still maintaining our Christian witness and allegiance to the true God? To what extent can we obey God and Caesar at the same time? Many wanted to maintain their Christian witness and hope, but also found Rome's promise of prosperity and flourishing irresistible! Rome promised peace, security, and financial stability to all who fell under its rule and acknowledged its power and greatness. Refusal to give the appropriate allegiance and worship to Rome could have a number of consequences: ostracism, verbal abuse, being perceived as seditious and uncooperative, and ungrateful for all that Rome had provided. For some it may have meant losing their job, their means of livelihood, or other forms of persecution. So far John only mentions one person who was martyred for his faith in Christ, a man named Antipas (2:13), but he thinks that the situation

9. Kraybill, *Apocalypse and Allegiance*, 57.
10. deSilva, *Unholy Allegiances*, 92.

will escalate and there will be more martyrdom on the horizon (see 6:9–11). At this stage in the history of the early church there was no widespread or official Roman persecution of Christians. The popular picture of Roman armies marching through cities and dragging Christians into the streets, or watching them torn apart by wild animals in the amphitheatre or beheaded, would only come later. At this point in time persecution was more sporadic and came at a local level from the city officials and neighbors, and often took the form of verbal assaults and accusations, or loss of economic benefits. But for John all this charts a course for the church, where it will clash with Rome and the world.

The other option was that Christians could choose to compromise with and attempt to accommodate to Roman rule, perhaps to avoid the suspicion, ostracism, and even economic consequences of refusing to bow down to Roman rule and religion. They would not want to be perceived as ungrateful, as bad citizens, or as rebellious. To what extent could Christians "serve two masters"? Rome's promise of wealth and economic prosperity would have been a temptation for many Christians living in these cities.[11] One common misunderstanding of Revelation is that it was written during a time when Christians were suffering widespread and extreme persecution, and John is writing to comfort and encourage them. However, when we read carefully the seven letters to the churches in chapters 2 and 3, it appears that the major issue is compromise and complacency (see below). Five of the seven churches (Ephesus, Pergamum, Thyatira, Sardis, Laodicea) are guilty of compromising to some degree with Rome and their pagan surroundings, and only two of the churches (Smyrna, Philadelphia) are marginalized and suffering any significant form of persecution. Against this backdrop John receives his vision and communicates it in the form of a letter to the churches in Asia Minor.

WHEN WAS REVELATION WRITTEN?

This leads to the question of when John saw his vision, wrote it down, and sent it to the seven churches in Asia Minor. While it is impossible to be certain, and their have been a number of suggestions for the precise date in the first century when Revelation was written, what we find in the book of Revelation itself is consistent with seeing Revelation as written towards the end of the first century during the reign of the Emperor Domitian (AD 95–96). Historically, an early church father named Irenaeus in the second

---

11. deSilva, *Unholy Allegiances*, 16.

century claimed that John had his vision towards the end of Domitian's reign. This has become the most popular dating for the book of Revelation.

Others have suggested that Revelation was written under the tyrannical emperor Nero (AD 60s). Some would point to the reference to seven heads-kings in Rev 17:10 as a clue to the date of Revelation. This text tells us that five heads (=emperors) have fallen, one is, and one is yet to come. If we can figure out which emperor John refers to with "one is," the one ruling when Revelation was written, then we could reasonably date Revelation. The problem is: 1) no one can agree where to start counting the seven emperors in v. 10 from the history of line of Roman emperors, which started with Julius Caesar; 2) seven is a symbolic number throughout Revelation, as it probably is here, so John likely does not have any specific "seven" in mind. Seven symbolizes the complete, totality of Roman emperors. Also, the number "seven" comes from Dan 7:1–7, where Daniel sees four beasts. If you count them, the total heads add up to seven, rather than from seven historical emperors.[12] Therefore, Rev 17:10 is of minimal help in determining who the ruling emperor was when John wrote, and therefore when Revelation was written. Though there is little clear evidence in Revelation itself that would point to a specific date, nothing in Revelation contradicts the testimony of Iranaeus, that it was written towards the end of Domitian's reign.[13] However, interpretation of any section of Revelation does not depend on our ability to date it with precision. We will assume the common dating of Revelation under the reign of Domitian around AD 95–96. What is the point of all this? Revelation was written in real space and time history, which can be identified in the book of Revelation itself. It was not about some fictional world, or some world far off in the distant future. Its location can be identified on a map. It was about the real world of everyday, first-century Christians living at a certain point in time under the most powerful empire of the day.

THE SEVEN CITIES IN REVELATION 2–3

The more specific details of the world of the book of Revelation can be found in the messages to the seven churches in chapters 2 to 3. Within the larger story of Roman rule and imperial worship (see above) were the individual stories of each of the seven cities that John addresses in these chapters. Each city had their own "story" about their struggle with Rome. These stories in chapters 2 to 3 are then retold in the form of an apocalyptic vision in the rest

12. deSilva, *Discovering Revelation*, 36.

13. Paul, *Revelation*, 16.

of the book of Revelation (4–22). Therefore, it is important to summarize the story of the seven cities and their churches. Revelation is not just about a fantasy world, nor is it about some world way off in the distant future (e.g., twenty-first century). It is about the world of the first-century Christians who were living out their lives in the context of the Roman Empire. In order to unlock the mysteries of the message of Revelation, we must understand the specific world of the seven churches which Revelation addresses. The stories of the seven churches and the issues they were facing living with the Roman Empire could be summarized as: pressure from within (from inside the church), and pressure from without (from outside the church).

Pressure from Within

Some of the churches in Rev 2–3 were experiencing pressures and conflicts inside of the Christian communities in these cities. The conflict was over the following issue: to what extent can we compromise with the Roman Empire? What is an acceptable level of accommodation with our surroundings? Can we participate in pagan meals and festivals in honor of the gods, and of the emperors? Can we give allegiance to Rome and its emperor, and at the same time worship God and the Lamb, especially if it means making a living and feeding my family? What would this look like? There were some in the churches who answered these questions in different ways. Some within the churches advocated compromising with the Roman economy and religion. It was acceptable to give allegiance to Rome and its emperor, to engage in activities and events in honor of the pagan Roman gods, and to prosper off Rome's economy. John singles out individuals and groups within the Christian communities who are responsible for such teaching. John points to one rival prophetess in the church of Thyatira that he calls "Jezebel" (2:21). This Jezebel was leading some Christians in the city of Thyatira into sin, teaching them to commit adultery and eat meat offered to idols. Eating meat offered to idols would have been part of the religious ceremonies and festivals in honor of the pagan gods, often in connection with trade and other economic associations. Refusal to participate would be seen as ungrateful or rebellious. Jezebel was spreading her propaganda that led Christians into compromising with their pagan surroundings and to show their allegiance to Rome. Jezebel was probably not her real name, but a name that John has given her based off an Old Testament figure. You can read the brief story about Jezebel that John was referring to in 1 Kgs 16:30–33. The queen Jezebel was responsible for leading Israel into idolatry and sin. She was also responsible for killing the prophets of the Lord (1 Kgs 18:4, 13). Therefore, like Jezebel in the Old Testament, this prophetess in the city of Thyatira was leading Christians astray by teaching them to accommodate with idolatrous Roman culture, values, and their economy. Perhaps she had a way of making what Rome had to offer look appealing.[14]

John refers to another group among the Christians, which he calls the "Nicolaitans," in 2:6 and 2:15. Who were these Nicolaitans? We cannot be certain of their precise identity, though the churches addressed in chapters 2 and 3 knew who they were. John warns Christians of the Nicolaitans' activities and teaching. They were probably a movement or group within the church advocating the same thing as the prophetess Jezebel: it is okay for Christians to accommodate with Roman culture. They were leading people in the church to compromise their faithful witness of the gospel of Jesus Christ by getting them to bow to the wishes of local officials and neighbors to show allegiance to the Roman emperor and its gods. Maybe they wanted the church to have a good standing with the local leaders and officials. This teaching is also identified as the teaching of Balaam (2:14), another Old Testament cipher for the teaching that it is acceptable for Christians to engage in feasts and other activities in honor of pagan gods and the emperor, such as eating meat that had been offered to idols. Balaam's story can be found in Num 22–24. In Num 31:16 he is portrayed as leading the Israelites astray. Like Balaam in the Old Testament, this teaching circulating in the church in Pergamum tried to lead Christians astray into idolatry and adultery (2:14). This adultery was probably spiritual, but may have included physical acts of sexual immorality. Once more, Christians were being tempted into compromising with their pagan surroundings so as not to appear renegades or as bad citizens. Therefore, Christians faced significant pressure from within their midst, from the church itself, to conform to Roman culture and practices, and so to compromise their faith in Jesus and witness to him.

Pressure from Without

The churches that John addressed in Rev 2–3 were also facing pressure from outside of the Christian community.[15] John himself was the object of pressure by the authorities in Asia Minor, who banished him to the island of Patmos for preaching the gospel (1:9), to them a threatening message. We have already considered the pressure that Christians in the broader communities of the seven churches would have faced, pressure by local officials and authorities to participate in veneration of pagan gods and emperors.

14. Culy, *Book of Revelation*, 115.
15. deSilva, *Discovering Revelation*, 82.

Often, one's position in society or ability to participate in Roman economy depended on this. In order to engage in business practices Christians would have been pressured to shown their loyalty and gratitude to the gods and to Rome. For example, there would have been ample opportunities to participate in festive meals and other occasions where the gods were worshiped or the emperor was venerated. Refusal to conform could bring serious consequences. The situation Christians faced can perhaps be seen most clearly in 2:10, where John tells the church in Smyrna to expect suffering in the form of being thrown into jail. This was probably not something that the emperor himself was enforcing, but local authorities and officials who harassed and persecuted Christians who refused to conform and show allegiance to Rome and its emperor (John refers to the ultimate instigator of such mistreatment as Satan himself!).

Another external pressure came from the Jewish synagogue. In two of the messages to the churches in Rev 2–3 John refers to "blasphemy from those who call themselves Jews and are not, but are of the synagogue of Satan" in the city of Smyrna (2:9) and to those in Philadelphia "from the synagogue of Satan, who call themselves Jews, but are not and are lying" (3:9). Why does John single out the Jewish synagogue, and why does he refer to them in this way? It appears that both churches were undergoing verbal harassment by the Jewish community there. Probably much of it was over the Christians' claim that Jesus was the Messiah. But how could a criminal crucified on a Roman cross for treason be the Messiah? These Christian communities were NOT the true people of God, according to those belonging to the Jewish synagogue. It is also possible that the reference in 2:9 to the Jews slandering Christians means that members of the Jewish community were bringing charges against Christians before the local officials and authorities, getting them in trouble and leading to further harassment and even prison.[16] By calling them the synagogue of Satan, John is not being nasty or vindictive, or playing a game of "name calling." He is pointing out once more the true source of the Christian communities' suffering: it is ultimately Satan himself who stands behind such attempts. The Jewish community, instead of acting like a synagogue, is taking the side of Satan, the accuser of the brothers and sisters (12:10), by inflicting suffering on Christians through their verbal assaults and even pointing an accusing finger before local authorities.[17]

The first-century church found itself in a dire situation indeed. They were between a proverbial "rock and a hard place." They faced pressures

16. Weima, *Sermons to the Seven Churches*, 69–72.
17. Paul, *Revelation*, 85.

from outside of and inside of the church that tempted them to compromise their faithful witness to Christ and his gospel. When we read the messages to the seven churches more carefully, it appears that the churches followed two different responses to these pressures and temptations to participate in the Roman culture and practices. Two of the churches refused to give in to the pressure to compromise, and they suffered the consequences. They are the harassed and persecuted church. But a more serious problem can be seen with the other five churches: they all compromised with their pagan surroundings or had become complacent to some degree. Each of the churches has their own story of navigating life in the midst of a pagan empire and pressures to conform.

"IN THE WORLD BUT NOT OF THE WORLD": THE HARASSED AND PERSECUTED CHURCH

Two of the churches addressed in chapters 2 to 3 were undergoing some level of persecution and marginalization, probably because of refusal to bow to the pressure to participate in the events and occasions associated with worship of the pagan gods, the emperor, and refused to immerse themselves in Roman culture and become wealthy off Rome's economy. As Jesus prayed for his disciples, they were "*in* the world but not *of* the world" (John 17:11, 14, 16). Because of this they were suffering the consequences of their decision. Jesus's evaluation of these two churches is positive, praising them for taking a stand. The two churches were found in the ancient cities of Smyrna and Philadelphia. The church situated in Smyrna (2:8–11) is assured by Jesus that he is aware of their affliction and poverty (v. 9), most probably because of refusal to conform to the pressures of participating in the Roman economy, which was exploitative and idolatrous.[18] Therefore, they suffered poverty as a result. Jesus also anticipates that they will suffer further and be thrown into prison (v. 10).

But they have received a "double whammy." They were also facing the slander of the Jewish synagogue (v. 9) which probably consisted of verbal assaults. The Jews in the city would not have considered Christians as true people of God, because they did not observe the Old Testament law, and believed that this crucified Jesus of Nazareth was the Messiah![19] Furthermore, those in the synagogue may have desired to distance themselves from Christians due to suspicion by the city that they were rebellious and refusing to conform. But the slander may also have involved accusation before the city

18. deSilva, *Unholy Allegiances*, 85.
19. deSilva, *Unholy Allegiances*, 88; Koester, *Revelation and the End of All Things*, 68.

officials and drawing attention to this new-fangled religion. Likewise, the church in the city of Philadelphia (3:7–13) is also receiving the same two-pronged attack as the church in Smyrna: local authorities and the Jewish synagogue. First, the church is described and having little power (v. 8). Their refusal to conform to local pressure to accommodate with Roman rule and worship of pagan gods has left them with no influence and financially destitute because of inability to participate in the Roman economy (remember, Roman economy and religion were closely intertwined!). They also faced hostility from the Jewish synagogue. Those of the synagogue disputed with Christians over belief that Jesus was the Messiah, and perhaps they wished to further distance themselves from Christians who were seen as rebels and refusing to conform. For these two churches, the book of Revelation would primary be a word of encouragement and comfort.

"IN THE WORLD AND OF THE WORLD": THE COMPLACENT AND COMPROMISING CHURCH[20]

The other five churches that Jesus addresses (Ephesus, Sardis, Thyatira, Pergamum, Laodicea) have compromised to some extent with their pagan, Roman surroundings, or have become complacent in their existence in the world. In contrast to Jesus's prayer for his followers, they were both "*in* the world" and "*of* the world" (John 17:11, 14, 16). Jesus's words to these churches are primarily negative, or a combination of praise and criticism. The city of Ephesus, an important commercial and urban center in Asia Minor, receives a mixed critique by Jesus (2:1–7). Although the church had not given into the temptation to worship pagan gods and had also resisted the infiltration of false teachings into their midst (vv. 1–3, 6), all was not well in the Ephesian church: they had forsaken their first love (v. 4). For what or whom had they lost their first love? Other Christians? Jesus himself? Unfortunately, we are "reading someone else's mail" some two-thousand years after it was written! So it is not crystal clear to us. But most likely it is their *love for Christ* that has grown cold and caused them no longer to be a faithful witness for Christ.[21] Perhaps they were good at maintaining doctrinal purity and religious observances, but they were not actively witnessing for Christ. This accounts for Christ's warning that if they do not repent he will remove their lampstand. The lampstand was a symbol of their witness to the world—they were to be a light to the world (see Matt 5:14–16). In the midst of all their activities and service for the sake of Christ, they have neglected

20. Koester, *Revelation and the End of All Things*, 61–67, 70–74.
21. Culy, *Book of Revelation*, 28–31.

their passionate love for him and ceased to actively witness to their worldly surroundings. They had grown complacent and were therefore ineffective in their witness for Christ.

When Christ examines the church in Sardis (3:1–6), another important commercial center and home of many pagan religions, he announces that the church is dead. Obviously, Jesus is referring to their spiritual status, since they were alive to hear this book read to them. The problem is that they have a reputation of being alive (v. 1). In the eyes of those in the city of Sardis, the church was prospering, accommodating, and fitting right in with the culture. They caused little offense in the eyes of the world. They had so assimilated into the surrounding culture that they even had a good reputation in the eyes of their neighbors. They were careful not to "rock the boat." But Jesus's words indict them for being spiritually dead, despite outward appearances, because they had compromised with their pagan surroundings.[22] They claimed to be Christians, but their lack of works to back up their claim, especially by assimilating to their pagan surroundings, rendered them spiritually dead. The churches found in two other cities, Pergamum (3:12–17) and Thyatira (2:18–29), had in common that they were affected by a teaching that had infiltrated the churches and encouraged accommodation with pagan Roman culture, religion, and economy. Both cities were centers of pagan religion and worship.

Pergamum in particular was a hotbed of pagan religion and emperor worship. The reference to Satan's throne could refer to the alter of Zeus in Pergamum,[23] but probably more generally to pagan religion and emperor worship at home in the city. Thyatira in particular would have had trade associations that Christians would have found it beneficial or necessary to belong to for prospering and thriving. These trade associations would have required participation in worship of pagan gods. John labels this teaching to accommodate with Rome and its religion and economy as the teaching of Balaam (v. 14) or the teaching of the Nicolaitans (v. 15). He also attributes this teaching to a rival female prophet that he calls "Jezebel" (v. 20). This teaching had one main focus: one could give allegiance to both Caesar and the Lord at the same time. It was okay and perhaps wise for Christians to accommodate. It was okay to participate in Rome's economy and even in the worship of the gods and emperor that often accompanied economic involvement. They were taught that it was acceptable to eat meat that had been offered to idols in the setting of temple meals or other festive occasions

22. Weima, *Sermons to the Seven Churches*, 174–75.

23. Weima, *Sermons to the Seven Churches*, 95–96.

(vv. 14, 20).[24] They were being led astray to commit adultery, spiritually but maybe also physically. Perhaps this teaching promoted peaceful existence among the unbelieving neighbors and local authorities, in order to avoid appearing rebellious and as bad citizens. This would also allow Christians to flourish in Rome's economic system. The messages to Pergamum and Thyatira make it clear that not all Christians there had fallen for this teaching, but many had.

The final church that was probably the worst off of all was the church in the city of Laodicea (3:14–22). Laodicea also had temples and shrines to pagan gods. And it apparently had especially benefited from the Roman economy.[25] Christ has no commendation for the church in Laodicea at all. First, they are "lukewarm" instead of "hot" or "cold" (vv. 15–16). Some people have interpreted this as a reference to spiritual temperature. Hot meant on fire for Christ, cold meant cold toward or rejecting Christ. Lukewarm was an in-between, uncommitted, middle-of-the-road Christianity. However, we need to understand these images in light of what they would have meant to the first readers. Hot and cold were both positive images, reflecting the hot water of nearby Hierapolis and the cold water of nearby Colossae. It may also picture a banquet setting, where hot and cold drink were desirable. In any case, hot and cold are both good things. Lukewarm may have reflected Laodicea's own water supply, or the idea that in the ancient world lukewarm water was undesirable for drink or was used to induce vomiting. Whatever the case, lukewarm is not a good thing (it is opposite of both hot and cold).[26] It would be similar to our experience in our favorite restaurant. Why does the waiter or waitress keep filling up our water glass, or topping off our coffee mug? Because we like drinks hot or cold. Noone likes lukewarm or tepid coffee or water. Lukewarm drink is disgusting and undrinkable. Second, Jesus further explains in what way the Laodicean church is lukewarm in the next verse (v. 17). They are rich and wealthy from Roman trade, and do not need anything. They have benefited from immersing themselves in Roman culture, religion, and the idolatrous economy, and now they have become so self-sufficient and arrogant, that they have no need of Christ. In other

24. Weima, *Sermons to the Seven Churches*, 103.

25. deSilva, *Unholy Allegiances*, 96.

26. For the background of hot, cold, and lukewarm in Laodicea, see Koester, *Revelation*, 343–44; Mathewson, *Companion to the Book of Revelation*, 53–55. It is wrong to take hot as spiritually hot, and cold as indifferent or spiritually cold, with lukewarm being "middle of the road." This popular misconception misses the associations that first century readers living in Laodicea in Asia Minor would have made. Furthermore, Laodicea is anything but middle-of-the-road. They are so compromising and self-sufficient that they have turned against Christ and are undrinkable and disgusting. They are the worst off of all the churches.

words, the Laodicean Christians are not uncommitted, middle-of-the-road Christians, but are living a thoroughly pagan and godless lifestyle that values wealth, achievement, and pride. That is what it means to be "lukewarm."

This quick survey of the problems in the seven churches summarizes the story that forms the backdrop for the rest of the book of Revelation. The seven messages in chapters 2 to 3 reveal seven actual, historical churches in the first century, whose individual stories can be located within the broader story of the Roman world of that day. At stake with all the churches was their faithful witness in the midst of a godless empire. This is the story and the issues that John addresses as a prophet in the rest of the book of Revelation.

CONCLUSION

So did anything really happen? Indeed it did! Behind the vision of Revelation and all the strange images lies the story of seven historical churches, each faced with the question of how to live out their faithful witness in the midst of a pagan, godless, idolatrous, and oppressive empire. It was an empire that claimed to be eternal, to be chosen by the gods, to offer peace, security, and prosperity to all who came under its rule. At the center of Roman life was the emperor, who took his place alongside the other Greek and Roman gods (at least in the eyes of cities and local officials). And Christians in the seven churches were facing pressure from within and pressure from without to conform to demands to show allegiance to and gratitude towards Rome and its emperor in the form of worship and allegiance. Christians who refused often experienced harassment and persecution, even imprisonment. In addition they faced verbal abuse and even accusations from local Jewish synagogues. Two of the churches John addressed (Smyrna and Philadelphia) had gone this route. But the far greater problem with the seven churches is that of complacency and compromise. Five of the churches fell within this category. Most of them, to avoid the consequences of refusing to accommodate, chose to give in to the pressure to conform and to participate in imperial life and economy. One church in particular, Laodicea, had prospered off Roman economy, and had become self-sufficient and proud. This is the story that lies behind the vision of Revelation and that John addresses in his apocalyptic-prophetic letter.

John's prophecy, letter, and apocalypse are a response to this real crisis in the seven churches (and other churches) within the Roman province of Asia. That is, Revelation is rooted in a real, historical situation. It is not fantasy literature with no connection to any known world or time period. It is not just a well-written literary portrayal of the battle between good and evil (though there is some truth to this; see next chapter), nor is it about some time and place far off in the distant (twenty-first century) future. It is about John, his first-century readers, and their world. And the book of Revelation was written to help them make sense of this world described above. This story provides an anchor in reading Revelation. It keeps us tethered to the first-century setting that John was addressing, so that we do not drift out into a sea of speculation and fanciful interpretations that end up reflecting our own experiences, political situations, and technologies. It is tempting to read the vision in 4:1—22:5 as something separate from the messages to the churches in 2–3, something that refers to a time and place long after the events in those churches. However, the rest of the book of Revelation, the "vision proper" in 4–22, will repeat the same message and refer to the same time period as the messages to the seven churches.[27] At the same time, it places the time period and location of the churches within a larger time period. It expands the world of the readers to include the entire earth and heaven (see Rev 4–5), and the time of the readers to extend backwards to the first creation (Gen 1–2) and forward to the future when Christ will return to bring final judgment and salvation (see Rev 19–22). The messages to the seven churches are supported and driven home to the readers by the vision in 4–22. If chapters 2 to 3 are a straightforward prophetic warning and encouragement to the churches, chapters 4 to 22 is the same message to those same churches but now in the form of an apocalyptic vision. The vision in 4–22 is the churches' story in a new key. The vision places the first century church within a broader story, a story that involves heaven, the whole creation and the battle between God and Satan, and the wrap-up of God's purposes at the end of history (see ch. 4 below).

The careful reader can see the situation of the historical seven churches reflected throughout 4–22. The seven seals in 6:1–11 are God's judgment on the unjust, godless economy in Rome (or any such economy) that thirsts for power and wealth at all costs, the very economy that Laodicea has grown rich from (3:17). These seals demonstrate what happens when God judges such an economy and system by allowing it to reap its own consequences. The two witnesses in Rev 11 recall the two faithful witnessing churches of Smyrna and Philadelphia, and the fact that the two witnesses are two lampstands recalls the lampstands in John's vision in chapter 1, which Jesus identifies as the seven churches (v. 20). The name Babylon in chapters 17 to 18 would have been a "code" for Rome in the first century. Chapter 18 further exposes the godless and idolatrous economy of Rome (Babylon) as the

27. See Culy, *Book of Revelation*, who takes the reader through the book of Revelation seven times, each time from the perspective of one of the seven churches in chs. 2–3.

reason for its judgments. The goods listed in Rev 18:11–13 were all staples of trade in the Roman economy which tempted churches such as Laodicea. The fact that Babylon-Rome was enticing others to "commit adultery" by participating in her unjust, godless economic and religious life, reflects the accusation of the prophetess Jezebel that she is leading Christians to "commit adultery" (2:20, 21). The reference to the "false prophet" in 16:13 and 19:20 recalls the "false prophetess" Jezebel in 2:20, who preaches a message of compromise to the churches.

Even the promises to the one who overcomes at the end of each message comes straight from the final vision of judgment and salvation when Christ returns in chapters 19 to 22. For example, the church in Ephesus is promised the tree of life in the paradise of God (2:7), which reflects the end-time tree of life in the final vision in 22:2. In other words, these connections show that the vision of 4–22 is anchored in the historical situation of the seven churches in 2–3. John's vison is not adrift at sea, tossed about by the waves of the reader's imagination. The vision of 4–22 was meant to shed light on the first readers' world and situation and can only be understood in light of what was going on in the seven churches.

PUTTING IT INTO PRACTICE

So what is it like to read Revelation with the ancient story of the seven churches and the Roman world in mind? We can see the story of the seven churches in Revelation and their historical situation reflected in the vision of the Dragon and two Beasts in Rev 12–13. At first glance this chapter reads more like a scene out of *Jurassic World*! But it tells a real story. The key actors are a woman (and her children), a child, a dragon (ch. 12), and two beasts (ch. 13). The woman symbolizes the people of God, both before the birth of Christ (vv. 1–4) and after the birth of Christ (vv. 6, 13–17). The dragon is unmistakably Satan, identified as the serpent who deceived Adam and Eve way back in the garden in Genesis 3 (v. 9). The son is clearly Jesus Christ, who is delivered from the deadly attempt of the dragon and taken to heaven (v. 5). Here Revelation clearly refers to a *past* event, not a future one. Frustrated with not being able to kill the son of the woman, the dragon goes after the woman and eventually her offspring (v. 17). The woman is preserved by being taken into the desert, a place of refuge and protection (vv. 6, 13). But her children are more vulnerable and suffer the wrath of the dragon (v. 17). What is going on here? The woman and her offspring both symbolize the church, the people of God, especially those in the seven cities struggling under the oppressive hand of Rome. That the women's children refer to the church, the people of God, is clear from the reference to them as those who keep the commandments of God and hold to their witness for Jesus (v. 17), the very thing the churches are called to do in chapters 2 and 3. The woman and her children look at the church from two different perspectives. The fact that the woman is preserved in the desert symbolizes the church's spiritual protection and preservation by God. But the fact that her children are vulnerable suggests that the church is not immune to physical suffering and persecution.

A key piece of the story is that the dragon has already been defeated by the death of Jesus Christ, and even knows that his time to wreak havoc is short (vv. 7–12). The people of God face a defeated foe, who doesn't have much time left to unleash his fury. The focus on the dragon, Satan, in this chapter recalls the references to Satan in chapters 2 and 3. Twice John refers to the synagogue of Satan (2:9; 3:9), Pergamum is the place where Satan's throne dwells (2:14), and Thyatira is warned of the "deep things of Satan" (2:24). The fact that the Jews are responsible for slandering the Christians in Smyrna (2:9) is reflected in Satan's role as the accuser of believers (12:10). In all of these instances, Jesus is uncovering (the meaning of "apocalypse"!) the true source of the churches' harassment, persecution, and temptations to compromise: it is Satan! Chapter 12, then, reveals in more detail the ultimate source of the churches' trouble: it is Satan's attempt to destroy the people of God, that goes all the way back to Jesus himself and even further to the very beginning, the temptation of Adam and Eve to sin (Gen 3). And this dragon has already been dealt a death blow by the death of Jesus Christ. All in all, chapter 12 is a further commentary on what the churches in chapters 2 and 3 are going through. At the same time, it places the situation of the churches in a broader story that goes all the way back to creation, and to the death of Christ, in order to shed fresh light on the first-century churches' troubles.

But Satan does not work solo. His two partners in crime are introduced to us in chapter 13 in the form of two beasts. In fact, both beasts are linked back to the dragon, and even are described like him. So the dragon, Satan, is the true commander behind these two beasts. Basically, they make life difficult for the people of God for their refusal to participate in the pagan culture and religious practices, and impose economic sanctions for their non-participation, symbolized by taking the mark of the beast (13:18). The first beast is given authority by the dragon, Satan, and commands universal worship. The second beast's job is to promote (demand?) the worldwide worship of the first beast. But who do these two beastly figures represent? Most likely, if you are a first-century reader, the first beast represents the Roman Empire and/or emperor, the world ruler of that day. The second beast represents the local officials and authorities in the seven cities that encourage allegiance to Rome and its emperor and even impose economic consequences on those who refuse to identify with Rome and show their loyalty to it (vv. 18).

In other words, chapters 12 and 13 explore in more detail the true nature of and the driving force behind the mistreatment of the church and the temptations to compromise in chapters 2 and 3. The image of a beast has a long Old Testament history of referring to anti-godly, oppressive, evil empires (Isa 27:1; 51:9; Dan 7:1–7). Now that same beastly character that inspired nations in the past can be found in the Roman Empire of John's day. And behind all of this ultimately lies the dragon, Satan, himself (ch. 12). The harassment, persecution, slander, and temptation to compromise are all Satanically inspired! Rev 12–13 are not a fantastic, fictional story of dragons and beasts. It is not a scene out of *Jurassic World*. Nor is it a prediction of some distant world and period of time, far off in the twenty-first century (or later). Rather, it is an uncovering of a real world and historical situation in the first century churches of Asia Minor. As an apocalyptic-prophetic work, it is meant to help the readers see their situation in a new light and to respond accordingly: with patient and faithful endurance for those who are harassed and persecuted, but repentance in the form of distancing from Roman religion and economy for those who are complacent and compromising. The next chapter will explore in more detail the main purposes of Revelation in light of the type of literature that it is and in light of the historical situation that it addresses.

Key #3

GOD'S SECRET AIMS
IN THE BOOK OF REVELATION

What was John Up To?

IF YOU MENTION THE book of Revelation in almost any setting, it immediately conjures up notions of visions of the end of the world. In the hands of most readers of the last book of the Bible, Revelation is nothing more than a prediction of events in the distant future. The primary aim of John in the book of Revelation was to predict the future and lay out a detailed course of events leading up to and including the second coming of Jesus at the end of history. This approach to Revelation portrays John as sort of a fortune teller who looks into a crystal ball and foretells the future for the inquiring Christian. Revelation is primarily a book about "eschatology" (teaching about the end-times). The book of Revelation has inspired countless "end-time" charts that meticulously map out the future events with detailed precision, to satisfy our curiosity of what the future holds in store and how close we might be to the end! There almost seems to be an inherent fascination in Christians with what the future holds. And Revelation seems to be just the book that promises to provide the answers to our questions about what is in store.

I remember growing up in church as a boy, listening to countless "prophecy experts" skilfully decode the book of Revelation by showing how its visions "matched up" with modern-day political, economic, and technological realities. I felt a mixture of both excitement and fear as I heard preacher after preacher unveil the end-time scenario for me. The mark of the beast, the number "666," was already making its way into our economic system. The political situation was shaping up for a final showdown in the Middle East. A one-world government was on the horizon, and a single currency was just around the corner. And all of these could be seen as predicted in the book of Revelation, and all pointed to the coming of Christ and the end of this world. Revelation was the Christian's "road map" to the future! The assumption behind this approach was that Revelation is primarily a prediction of end-time events that awaited decoding by modern-day prophets. John's main concern was to foretell the future. But is this what Revelation is really all about? Is the last book of the Bible nothing more than the prediction of an end-time scenario, a detailed road map of the future? A crucial key to unlocking the treasures of the apocalypse is to figure out what the book of Revelation was trying to accomplish. Like any other book in the New Testament, Revelation has a specific purpose (or purposes). What were God's aims in the book of Revelation? What was John really up to?

GETTING OUR BEARINGS STRAIGHT

The aims of God in Revelation, through his prophet John, grow out of the kind of literature that Revelation is and the historical situation that John was addressing. In the first chapter we saw that Revelation belonged to a kind of literature that would have been familiar to the first readers. It actually belonged to three different literary types: apocalypse, prophecy, and letter. A key feature of these types of literature is that they directly addressed the readers' situation to help them make sense of what was going on. As an apocalypse Revelation is unveiling the readers' world so that they can see it in a new light and change their perspective and lives accordingly. As a prophecy, Revelation is not primarily about *foretelling* (predicting the future), but *forthtelling*, communicating a message of encouragement but also warning to the present time of the readers. As a letter, Revelation is addressing the specific needs of the first readers and communicating something to them that would make sense of the problems they are facing and that they would understand. Even though prediction of the future did play a role in apocalypses and prophecies, that was not their main function, and even visions of the future were meant to inspire the people of God in their present time. In the last chapter we saw that Revelation was not some fantasy literature, or a prediction of a future world off in the distant future. John does not just have a vision out of thin air. His vision was in response to the current situation of seven historical churches in the first-century Roman province of Asia Minor. Their situation is spelled out in some detail in the seven messages to those churches in chapters 2 and 3. Revelation was addressed to Christians facing the challenges of living out their faithful witness in the midst of a godless, idolatrous, oppressive empire. Therefore, our understanding of the purpose and aims of Revelation must be consistent with the type of literature that Revelation is, and the historical context in which it was written. We must pay close attention to the book of Revelation itself to see what it reveals about its purpose. So why did God give this vision to John to record for the seven churches to hear?

WHAT REVELATION IS ALL ABOUT

Inspire Hope

While reading the book of Revelation as a crystal ball through which John could see the distant future is a misguided pursuit, there is at least a kernel of truth in this approach: Revelation does refer to the final wrap-up of history to inspire hope in the people of God. The message of Revelation is that one day God will intervene and set things right. He will right all the wrongs that God's people experience in this world. Revelation is not a "road map" of the future, but that does not mean it has no interest in the future. It does. The visions of the future are a means of alternatively encouraging and warning the people of God in the present. There is still some *foretelling*, even if its primary aim as a prophecy is *forthtelling*. The foretelling looks to a day when God will intervene into the affairs of this world, reward his faithful people, bring judgment of his enemies, remove sin and all the effects of evil, renew all of creation, and establish his reign throughout the entire cosmos. Without a resolution in the future, the present would be meaningless. John's main aim in the book of Revelation is not to give a detailed timeline or exhaustive map of how or when all these events will occur, and in what order. John is not attempting to satisfy his readers' curiosity about what the future holds. Instead, John writes to provide a vision of a future hope meant to inspire God's people toward faithful living and perseverance in the midst of adversity. John writes to assure his readers that these things will happen, not exactly when or how they will happen! God will send his Messiah to climax God's redemptive promises for his people and for all creation.

In the very first chapter John signals his intent to assure is readers that history is building to the ultimate goal of the coming of Christ to bring salvation and judgment. John bookends his work with references to the coming of Christ at the end of history to consummate God's redemptive plan. In 1:7 John anticipates a time when Christ will come in the clouds in a public display for all to see, and all peoples of the earth will mourn, probably a reference to many turning to Christ in repentance. Then he ends his book with Jesus himself promising to return soon (22:7, 12, 20). This promise to return soon refers to what theologians call the Second Coming of Christ at the end of history. In promising that his coming is "soon" Jesus is not predicting that he would return in the first century. Jesus is expressing the common belief of the early church: Christ *could* come back at any time, even in their lifetime. This does not require that he necessarily *will*, but that he *could*. Jesus's concern is not to predict the time of his coming, but to foster vigilance and obedience in light of the fact that Christ could come back at any time. These three promises of Christ's soon return are in the context of ethical exhortation to obedience and faithfulness.[1]

After chapter 1, John often anticipates the end-time return of Christ to bring God's redemptive plan in salvation and judgment to completion. Several times John refers to the future coming of Christ to bring judgment and salvation, but in a way that only wets our appetite for a fuller vision of the end of all things. At the end of the sequence of seals in Rev 6, the sixth seal brings the reader to the brink of the end:

> I watched as he opened the sixth seal. There was a great earth-quake. The sun turned black like sackcloth made of goat hair, the whole moon turned blood red, and the stars in the sky fell to earth, as late figs drop from a fig tree when shaken by a strong wind. The sky receded like a scroll, rolling up, and every mountain and island was removed from its place (6:12–14).

This language of the catastrophic happenings and the breakup of the constellations comes from the Old Testament (Isa 34:4; Joel 2:31), and symbolically refers to the effects of Christ's return in the future. This is not a literal description, but symbolically describes the "earth shaking" effects of the return of Christ to earth. We sometimes use the expression "she turned the world upside down" to describe the momentous results of someone's actions, without suggesting that they literally flipped the earth on its axis. The response of the inhabitants of the earth identifies this as the Day of the wrath of the Lamb (vv. 16–17), where God pours out his judgment on wicked humanity at the end of history. The opposite perspective on the future coming of Christ is found in chapter 7, where an innumerable multitude stands before the throne of God, having coming through the period of tribulation. They now stand victorious in God's presence, and experience life in the future new creation (see Rev 21–22). Both of these visions inspire hope in God's people, that God will one day set things right by judging their enemies (ch.

1. See Mathewson, *Where is the Promise of His Coming?*, 77–96.

6) but rewarding his faithful people (ch. 7). Again, these visions whet the readers' appetite for a fuller description of the wrap up of God's plan of redemption. Chapter 14 alternates between visions of judgment and salvation, still leaving the reader with a desire for a further unveiling of the end-time coming of Christ. All of these initial visions of the future point to the fullest expression of God's future salvation and judgment at the end-time coming of Christ in Rev 19–22.

John's most extensive vision of end-time judgment occurs in 19:11—20:15. The final judgment centers on the three diabolical characters introduced in chapters 12 and 13: the Dragon and the two Beasts. They are disposed of in the reverse order they were introduced in chapters 12 and 13. Rev 19:11–21 records the judgment of the two beasts from chapter 13 in an end-time battle by Christ who is depicted as a rider on a white horse. This is no typical battle in that no actual fighting takes place, but the beasts and those who follow them are simply destroyed in judgment. Chapter 20 then records the judgment of Satan from chapter 12. He is first of all locked in an abyss, again a symbol of judgment, only to be let out to go into final judgment in the lake of fire with his two beastly cohorts. The final destiny of the beasts, the dragon, and their followers is the lake of fire, a real place of punishment but depicted symbolically by the lake of fire . He is defeated in an end-time battle, probably the same battle as chapter 19 where the beasts were defeated. It is the same battle from two different perspectives: the defeat of the beasts, and the defeat of Satan. There then follows a comprehensive judgment of everything, including the present creation, in 20:12–15. This is the final "sweeping up" of all things in a final judgment. This "great white throne" judgment is probably to be understood as the judgment of all unbelievers. The point is that by the end of chapter 20, everything that stands in opposition to God, his people, and the fulfillment of his redemptive purposes, has been removed in the final judgment. The point is not to give a detailed time-line or chronological account or road map of the future, but to assure God's people that one day God will indeed remove everything in judgment that stands opposed to the establishment of God's kingdom and his people's enjoyment of it. The removal of everything, including the present creation racked by sin and evil, now paves the way for the emergence of a new world (21:1—22:5) that will be the inheritance of God's people who were faithful despite what they have sacrificed or suffered on this earth.

After everything has been removed in judgment, John sees a "new heavens and new earth" (21:1), which replaces the old earth that has passed away in judgment. This new creation is the home of the new Jerusalem (v. 2), which symbolizes God's people themselves: The new Jerusalem is identified as the bride of the Lamb (vv. 9–10), which is the people of God in 19:7–9. The point of John's vision is that the final destiny of God's people is a new *earth*. That is, God's people are not destined to "float around on clouds in heaven," but are destined for existence on a physical earth, stripped of all the effects of evil and all the things that make life painful and difficult for God's people in the present. It will be like a return to the conditions of the garden of Eden (22:1–2; see Gen 2) Life, beauty, order, and whole-ness reign supreme in the new creation. No more injustice; no more death; no more pain, sorrow, and disappointment. The measurements of the new Jerusalem-people (e.g., 12,000, 144) are not meant to provide architectural details, but are all multiples of the number twelve, which is a number that symbolizes the complete, perfected people of God. John sees the people of God in their final, perfected redeemed state, living on a new earth. But the key point is not geography or human happiness. The most important fea-ture of this the final vision is that God and the Lamb are present with their people (21:22; 22:3). That is, God and the Lamb are at the center of the new creation and now live in the midst of them on a renewed earth. The focus is not on a place, but on a Person.

This vision of end-time salvation is not meant to fuel our speculation as to when these things will take place, or exactly what life will be like in the future. It is meant to inspire God's people to holy living in the present. If God is going to one day set all things right with the coming of his son Jesus Christ, then God's people should live responsibly in the present. To borrow the words of Peter: if the world is going to end in this way, "what kind of people ought you to be?" Answer: "You ought to live holy and godly lives" (2 Pet 3:11). The seven messages to the churches in Rev 2–3 each end with a promise taken from chapters 19 to 22. That is, the vision of end-time judgment and salvation in chapters 19 to 22 are meant to inspire the churches in their faithful witness to Christ and the gospel. If God's people are called on to resist Roman rule, to refuse to compromise with their pagan environment, and follow the Lamb no matter what they cost, if they are to "come out" of Babylon-Rome (18:4), they need a place to go. And the vision of the new creation and new Jerusalem provides them with a future hope, a future destination, and inspires them to persevere, or repent and follow the Lamb. So Revelation does foretell the future, but not for the purpose of giving the reader a detailed time line or road map of the future, or to satisfy our curiosity or predict when Christ will return. Rather, it is meant to help God's people make sense of their present, by inspiring hope in a future where God will one day set all things right. God's people will experience God and the Lamb's unending presence as the long-awaited goal of God's redemptive purposes. And our hope is not escape from this body and this world, to float in the heavenly clouds. Our destiny is a physical, bodily, and earthly existence, but stripped of all the effects of evil and sin that plague this current existence. Such a vision should make clinging to this present existence less desirable. And it compels God's people to reflect the life in the future new creation right now, in advance of its future arrival.

Encourage Obedience and Faithful Witness

The seven messages to the churches in Asia Minor in chapters 2 and 3 set the tone for the rest of the book of Revelation. They reveal the struggles of seven historical churches in the first century for whom John records this vision that he had. As we have already noted, the seven messages to the churches were primarily meant to encourage the church to maintain its faithful witness to Christ and to the reality of God's kingdom. Two of the churches in Asia Minor (Smyrna, Philadelphia) are suffering some level of persecution or harassment at the hands of local authorities and even local Jewish synagogues, and they are encouraged to persevere to the end and maintain their faithful witness.

But what is often missed is that calls to perseverance and faithful witness and obedience are sprinkled throughout the rest of the book. Consider the following passages scattered throughout the vision in chapters 4 to 22, which explicitly call on God's people to respond to the vision in faithful obedience and perseverance. They are sort of "commentary" on the vision, inserted at points by John to guide the readers in response to the vision:

> He who has an ear, let them hear. If anyone is to go into captivity, into captivity they will go. If anyone is to be killed with the sword, with the sword they will be killed. This calls for patient endurance on the part of the saints (13:9–10)

> This calls for patient endurance on the part of the saints who obey God's commandments and remain faithful to Jesus (14:12)

> Behold, I come like a thief. Blessed is the one who stays awake and keeps their clothes with them, so that they might not go naked and be shamefully exposed (16:15; the imagery of clothing standing for faithfulness and preparedness)

> Blessed and holy are those who have part in the first resurrection. The second death will have no power over them, but they will be priests of God and of Christ and will reign with him for a thousand years (20:6; this blessing is pronounced on those who participate in the first resurrection, who are identified as those who kept the testimony of Jesus and God's word [v. 4]).

All of these "reminders" are placed at crucial moments in the vision to call on God's people to respond with endurance in their obedience and faithful witness. They should have ears to hear the call of Revelation to faithful obedience. As such, they tell us what the visions are all about and what God's aims are in this vision he gives to John.

There are more indirect calls to obedience and faithful witness throughout the book. In chapter 11 John describes two witnesses, who carry out their witness in the face of opposition by the world. The two witnesses symbolize the entire church (see below). This can be seen by the fact that the two witnesses are identified as lampstands (v. 4). Back in 1:20 Christ himself had already identified the lampstands as the seven churches. The fact that there are only two is probably because only two of the churches in chapters 2 and 3 are faithful witness, and therefore suffering some form of harassment of persecution. The two faithful churches of Smyrna and Philadelphia represent and model what all the churches should be doing: maintaining their faithful witness even in the face of hostility and opposition by the world. Therefore, chapter 11 is not so much a prediction of the end times, but sort of a call for the church to fulfill its faithful witness, even in the face of opposition and suffering.

In the very next chapter, in 12:17 the children of the woman, who symbolize the church, the people of God are described as "those who obey God's commandments and hold to the testimony of Jesus." This is meant to be an implied encouragement to the church to follow this example: they should obey God's commands and maintain their testimony or witness to Jesus, even in the face of Satan's persecuting activity. Rev 14:4 provides the clearest summary of what John is trying to get his readers to do: the people of God, symbolized by the 144,000, are described as those who "follow the Lamb wherever he goes." Revelation is ultimately a book of discipleship. It is meant to get its readers to follow the way of Jesus. In Revelation Jesus himself is described as "the faithful and true witness" (3:14). Furthermore, the image of Jesus as the slain Lamb models what it means to follow Jesus wherever he goes: he goes the way of suffering, and even death, as a result of his faithful witness. Therefore, the church is called to reflect Jesus's faithful witness even to the point of death in their own lives. They are to faithfully witness to the truth of the gospel and reality of God's kingdom, no matter what the consequences it brings. In Jesus's case it meant death. And for at least one person in the city of Pergamum, a faithful witness named Antipas, it also meant death (2:13).

The call for obedience and faithful witness in the people of God is driven home most forcefully in the conclusion of the book: 22:6–22. This entire concluding section can be seen as sort of an instruction manual, or reading guide, to Revelation. It instructs the readers of the book on how they are to read it, what they are to do with it, and what their response should be. The instruction to God's people begins with a blessing for the one who keeps (obeys) John's book (22:7). This provides another "bookend" with 1:3, where a blessing is pronounced on the one who hears and keeps (obeys) John's prophetic book. That is, the entire books is encased within calls to obey the entire book, not just part of it. This includes the entire vision in chapters 4 to 22. The second instruction is in the form of a promise by Jesus Christ that at his coming he will reward everyone for what they have done, further motivating the churches to holy and obedient living (22:12–13). This is followed by another blessing in v. 14. This blessing in pronounced on those who wash their robes, a symbol of the purity, holiness, and obedience of the people of God. If they maintain their holiness in the midst of a corrupt world, they are promised entrance into the gates of the city (the new Jerusalem) and a share in the tree of life. Both of these feature in the final vision of salvation in 21:1—22:5, further proving that John's vision of end time salvation is meant to motivate godly living, persistent obedience, and faithful witness, not to satisfy our curiosity about the future.[2] On the flip side, those who do not obey and keep themselves pure will be excluded from life in the new creation and new Jerusalem (22:15).

A final call to obedience and faithfulness if found in 22:18–19. Here John warns against "adding to" and "subtracting from" the book of Revelation. Most interpreters have taken this as a warning not to tamper with the wording of Revelation, to provide additional verses, or to delete sections. Some have even taken it as a warning against adding or subtracting books from the New Testament. However, it is important to note that this warning is given to those who hear the words of Revelation read to them, the churches (v. 18). This is identical to the blessing given to those who hear the words of Revelation at the beginning of the book in 1:3. There, the one who was blessed was the one who heard and obeyed (kept) the entire book of Revelation. Here, the adding and subtracting are probably metaphorical for failing to keep the words of the book, or failing to obey it. To add to or subtract from Revelation means to refuse to heed its warnings, and to fail to obey and be faithful witnesses.[3] If 1:3 pronounces a blessing on the one who hears and obeys, 22:18–19 pronounce a curse on the one who hears and refuses to obey. John is referring to those who would "pick and choose" what they wanted to follow in the book of Revelation. Perhaps some of Revelation, particularly in the seven messages to the churches, could have been

2. Schüssler Fiorenza, *Revelation: Vision of a Just World*, 115.

3. Beale, *Revelation*, 1151–53.

offensive to some, so that parts of Revelation could be rationalized away or ignored. Whatever the exact case, the entire book of Revelation is bookended with calls to obedience and warnings against failure to do so. Revelation is not primarily predicting a course of future events or giving us a road map to the future, it is encouraging obedience and faithful witness in the people of God. If we miss that message, we have missed the point of Revelation. The calls to obedience are not limited to the messages to the churches in chapters 2 and 3, but extend to the entire vision in 4–22. In the New Testament and especially the book of Revelation, eschatology (teaching on the end-times) is always in the service of holiness. John's vision should stir God's people to perseverance in obeying God's commands and maintaining their faithful witness, even in the face of opposition and rejection, and competing claims to loyalty. After all, this is the way of Jesus Christ, the model faithful witness and obedient servant who died for his people. And God's people "follow the Lamb wherever he goes" (14:4).

Warn of Complacency and Compromise

The flipside of encouragement to obedience and faithful living is warning against complacency and compromise in the churches. As we have already noted, five of the seven churches in chapters 2 and 3 are guilty of some level of complacency or accommodation with the godless, evil, unjust Roman Empire. Ephesus has lost its first love. Some in Pergamum and Thyatira tolerate a wrong teaching that leads God's people to compromise and participate in pagan religious practices. Sardis is dead spiritually. Laodicea has become proud and self-sufficient because they have become successful and rich off Rome's economy. Therefore, the majority of the churches are spiritually sick, and John's diagnosis reveals a church in serious danger. This means that the main purpose of Revelation is not to comfort persecuted Christians, although it does that for two of the churches (Smyrna, Philadelphia).

The more pressing concern is to warn those churches who are complacent and compromising with the pagan surroundings and to call them to repent. For them, Revelation is a wake-up call to resist the allurement of what Rome has to offer, and to turn and become faithful witnesses for Christ, no matter what the consequences. Rome billed itself as the eternal city, the city chosen by the gods. It proclaimed its status and world-wide rule through a system of worship of the gods, but also of the emperor. Daily life in these cities was wrapped up in religious observance through participation in worshiping the gods and the emperor. Often, one's survival and success economically and socially depended on such participation, not least the need to appear as good citizens. A group called the Nicolaitans were advocating that Christians could compromise with their surrounding culture. A prophetess that John calls "Jezebel" is also leading Christians into thinking that they can compromise with the pagan Roman system to avoid the consequences that refusal to participate would bring. Revelation warns against the danger of such compromise and complacency.

More than likely, those five churches who were compromising and complacent would have read Revelation very differently from the two churches suffering harassment and persecution. It would have impacted them in a different way due to their background and circumstances of compromise and complacency. For example, while the two suffering churches would have read the scenes of judgment as vindication from their oppressors, the five compromising churches would have read them as warnings for them to avoid such judgments by repenting of their compromise. We have already seen that Revelation's visions of judgment may have reflected the Roman economic situation of the day. The six seals in 6:1–18 probably reflects God's judgment on a Roman economy built on thirst for wealth and prosperity. Something similar may be said about the trumpet (chs. 8–9) and bowl (ch. 16) judgments. They are attacks on the stability and order of life in this world. God's judgments undermine the normalcy of human life. They undermine humanity's objects of trust and dependence. And those in the churches are not immune from God's judgment if they persist in compromising and refusing to repent. Chapter 18 pictures Babylon/Rome's judgment because of her godless, murderous, arrogant, and idolatrous nature. The judgment is primarily voiced through three different groups that mourn her destruction, because they benefited economically and financially from her. The kings of the earth no longer share in her luxury (vv. 9–10). The merchants no longer have anyone to sell their goods to (vv. 11–17). Those who sail the seas and make a living through shipping goods no longer have any cargo to ship (vv. 17–20). Those in the churches are warned to "come out of her" (v. 4) so that they do not share in her judgment. This is the danger that faces the churches who are compromising, if they refuse to repent. This is especially pertinent to churches like Laodicea who have become rich off of the Roman economy so that they see no need for anything else.

The final judgment in 19:11–21 by the rider on the white horse (Jesus Christ) is directed against all rebellious humanity, consisting of all classes of people: "kings, generals, and mighty men, of horses and their riders, and all people, free and slave, small and great" (v. 18). That is, God's judgments will be comprehensive and no respecter of persons, no matter what their status. This would include anyone in the churches who compromise with Rome and side with the beast and the rest of humanity headed for judgment. They would not want to be on the wrong side of God's judgment. Revelation's vision would be a loud call for them to wake up and repent, in order to maintain their faithful witness to the Gospel, even at the risk of economic consequences because they do not participate in Rome's corrupt system and economy. Therefore, the visions of judgment in Revelation are not just predictions of an unavoidable fate and worldwide judgment in the future, but are a call to avoid this judgment by repenting and carrying out our faithful witness in the world. The judgment scenes are part of John's strategy to warn the complacent and compromising church.

For many readers of this book, persecution, at least in the form it is presented in Revelation, will likely never be an issue. But the temptation to compromise and complacency will be. Like it did in the first century, this world offers attractive options to faithfulness to God and Jesus Christ. Embracing our consumer-driven culture which promotes self-sufficiency and self-fulfillment, only mutes our ability to faithfully witness to the reality of God and his Son Jesus Christ. Revelation confronts us with a warning not to become complacent in this world, and not to compromise our faithful witness and obedience to "the commandments of Jesus Christ" (12:17). We need "ears to hear what the Spirit is saying to the churches." Revelation calls us to loosen our grip on the things of this world in order to obtain an eternal inheritance that far exceeds anything this world has to offer (21:1—22:5).

Inspire Worship of the True God

Did you know that Revelation is mainly a book of worship? This usually gets overlooked in approaches that see Revelation as nothing more than giving us information about what is going to happen in the future. But all you need to do is skim through the book of Revelation and notice all the places where groups or individuals sing songs in response to who God is and what he has done to see the important role that worship plays in this book. This is because one of the questions that Revelation addresses is: Who is truly worthy of worship? Who is the Lord of all and worthy of unqualified obedience? The readers of Revelation were confronted with alternative claims to allegiance. As noted in the previous chapter, John's readers lived in a religiously charged environment. The cities in which they lived were home to pagan gods, with altars and shrines devoted to the gods.[4] There were also altars and shrines in honor of the Roman emperor, and a system of emperor worship promoted by local authorities. Economics, politics, and

4. See Ascough, "Greco-Roman Religions and the Context of the Book of Revelation," 170–75 for a summary of the various religious cults in the seven cities.

religion would have been closely intertwined. It would be a sign of extreme disrespect and ingratitude not to show allegiance to and homage to the gods and the emperor, who were responsible for the peace and prosperity you enjoyed. To serve as a good citizen would mean participating in local religious observances.

So Christians faced pressure to conform to the cultural and religious pressure to show allegiance to the gods and the emperor; refusal to do so could cost them economically and in their social standing. One of John's purposes is to reorient his readers to the true object of worship: God and the Lamb. To worship the emperor or the Roman gods, or any other person, being, or entity is idolatry. Only God and the Lamb are worthy of the exclusive worship of their people. No one can serve two masters! Even the angels are not worthy of worship. Twice, John falls down to worship the angel showing him part of the vision, and twice the angel replies, "Do not do it! I am a fellow servant with you and with your brothers (the prophets) and those who hold to the testimony of Jesus/keep the words of this book. Worship (only) God!" (19:10; 22:9). Therefore, Revelation over and over raises the question: who is worthy of the worship of God's people? And John provides the answer to this question loud and clear.

The main vision of chapters 4 to 22 begins with a stirring scene of worship in chapters 4 and 5. In response to the question of who is truly worthy of worship, Rev 4 begins with a scene of the heavenly throne room, with the throne and God seated on it at the center. At the center of true reality is not Caesar and his throne, but God. The throne, a symbol of sovereignty and authority, occurs fourteen times in chapter 4, and another five times in chapter 5. The true throne is in heaven, not in Rome! A chorus of worship is sung by the four living creatures (probably angelic beings that represent the entire created order) who proclaim: "Holy, holy, holy is the Lord God Almighty, who was, and is, and is to come" (4:8). Likewise, a group of twenty-four elders (probably also angelic beings who represent the twelve tribes of Israel and the twelve apostles) sing: "You are worthy, our Lord and God, to receive glory and honor and power, for you created all things and by your will they were created and have their being" (v. 11). God is the eternal, sovereign ruler over all of creation and is the creator of all things, and therefore is worthy of the worship of the whole universe. Rev 4 stands as a counter-claim to Rome and its emperor. Chapter 4 calls Christians to resist the lure of idolatry, of worshiping the pagan gods and participating in the imperial cult. Such activities are idolatrous and contradict the exclusive worship of God alone. Activities such as prayers and sacrifices offered up to the emperor would have been common occurrences. Some cities organized male choirs that sung praises to the emperor. Ceremonies in honor of the emperor, such as celebrating his birthday, would be accompanied by crowns, incense, and lamps.[5] Perhaps the heavenly worship scene in chapters 4 and 5, then, is meant to deliberately contrast with this. John assures his readers that it is God who sits on the throne in heaven at the center of all reality. And the angelic choirs in heaven attend to him and sing words of praise and worship in heavenly procession. Bowls of incense are offered to the Lamb (5:8), not to Caesar.

The heavenly worship scene continues in chapter 5, but a new figure is introduced: the Lamb. This chapter also introduces us to a sealed scroll, which probably contains God's plan of establishing his kingdom on earth and his redemptive purposes. The question that the chapter raises is: who is worthy to unseal and open the scroll from v. 1? The answer: the slain Lamb is worthy. Jesus is the only one who is worthy to open the scroll and unleash its contents, God's redemptive plan. This evokes the praise and worship of heaven, in the same way God's sovereignty over creation evoke the worship of heaven in chapter 4. It would be more accurate to say that heaven erupts or explodes in worship when Christ takes the scroll! In ever-widening circles in chapter 5, heaven breaks out in worship of the Lamb, in terms similar to that give to God in chapter 4. God's redemptive activity in Jesus Christ in offering himself up as a sacrifice and purchasing people to be God's possession brings on the first response of worship: "You are worthy to take the scroll" (v. 9). A larger group also praises God because he is the slain Lamb (v. 12). And then finally all of heaven and earth, in universal chorus, worship the Lamb by ascribing praise, honor, glory, and power (v. 13): "To him who sits on the throne and to the Lamb be praise and honor and glory and power, for ever and ever!" What is intriguing in this last outburst of praise is that God and the Lamb now occupy the same throne and receive the same worship! The scene ends with the four living creatures and twenty-four elders falling prostrate and worshiping God and the Lamb (v. 14). The point of this heavenly scene is that God and the Lamb are worshiped because God is the creator of all, and through the Lamb is the redeemer of all. For that reason they are worthy of the worship of the entire universe! These two chapters set the stage for the rest of the book. It will draw God's people to worship God and the Lamb, and not any other being. God's people on earth are to join the heavenly chorus of praise. Revelation 4–5 calls on God's people to render exclusive allegiance to God and the Lamb in the face of competing claims of allegiance (Rome), no matter what the consequences. And God's people on earth worship God and the Lamb for the same reason they do in

5. Kraybill, *Apocalypse and Allegiance*, 60

heaven: God is worthy of worship because he is the creator of all and the redeemer of all.

In chapter 15 we are introduced to another song of worship, this time sung by the redeemed people of God. Drawing on Exodus imagery, Rev 15:1–4 portrays the people of God standing victorious in God's presence, and singing the song of Moses and the Lamb. In the Old Testament Moses and the Israelites sang of song in praise of God's deliverance of Israel from Egypt at the Red Sea. Now, the new people of God who believe in the Lamb, also stand by the sea and sing a song of worship to God for delivering them. The focus of the song is on God's sovereignty and his marvelous deeds shown in rescuing his people. The people respond:

> Great and marvelous are your deeds, Lord God Almighty.
>> Just and true are your ways, King of the ages.
> Who will not fear you, O Lord
>> For you alone are holy.
> All nations will come and worship before you,
>> for your righteous acts have been revealed (15:3–4)

Like the hymns in chapters 4 and 5, God's sovereignty and holiness shown by his mighty acts of redemption evoke a response of worship in the people of God.

The final scene of worship occurs in the vision of 21:1—22:5. In one sense, the heavenly scene of chapters 4–5 now becomes a reality on earth, as all the people of God, including people from all the nations, worship God and the Lamb whose throne is now at the center of the new creation (22:2, 3). The nations that were formerly under the sway of the beast and who served Rome, now bring their glory and honor into the new Jerusalem (21:24, 26). They now give their loyalty and allegiance to God and the Lamb. The people of God play a priestly role (22:4–5), serving God with their praise and worship. God and the Lamb are now at their rightful place in the center of the new creation, and all creation worships them in fulfillment of the vision of heavenly worship in chapters 4–5. Once again, the church in the present is called on to worship in anticipation of the future day when all creation will worship God in the new creation. From start (chapters 4–5) to finish (21:1—22:5), the scenes of worship reorient God's people towards the true center of reality and the only true object of worship

These are only examples of the prevalence of worship throughout Revelation. We could look at many more examples. But all the acts of worship throughout Revelation reflect the same concerns: God and the Lamb are praised and worshiped because of their mighty acts of judgment and salvation which reflect their just and holy character. Worship reorients

God's people back to the true center of reality, to the God who is seated on his throne, reminding God's people of the sovereignty and character of the One who is on the throne. It leads us with the hosts of heaven into the very presence of God. This is especially necessary in the face of competing claims by Rome and the cities in which Christians found themselves. The book of Revelation, with its stirring visions of worship, should continue to inspire the people of God today to worship God. Revelation has inspired countless worship songs, both old and new, in our church today. Jake Hamilton's "Beautiful Rider" draws on the vision of Christ from Rev 5 and 19. The words of John Thurlow's "Jesus You're Beautiful" comes from the vision of the exalted Christ in Rev 1:12–15. "The Revelation Song" by James Lee Riddle (sung by Kari Jobe and Gateway Worship) comes directly from Rev 4 and 5. The recent song by Andrew Peterson, "Is He Worthy!" is likewise inspired by Rev 5. This is in line with the main purpose of the book. Revelation should inspire worship. When we worship, we reorient ourselves and align ourselves with the true center of reality, God who is seated on the throne, and the Lamb. When we worship here on earth we join in heaven in acknowledging God's sovereignty and holy character, and the Lamb's worthiness to accomplish God's plan of redemption.

Critique Ungodly Nations and Empires

A final aim in the book of Revelation is to expose and critique the ungodly, idolatrous empire of John's day: Rome. As we saw in chapter 2 above, the seven churches lived under the imperial Roman regime. Rome proclaimed itself as "Eternal Rome" which brought peace, prosperity, and salvation to all who came under its rule. Rome was chosen by the gods, and at the center of all reality. It maintained and asserted its importance through a system of religious observance in the form of temples and altars to pagan gods and to the emperor. But one of the things that John does in Revelation is unveil the true nature of Rome. This is the meaning of "apocalypse," an uncovering, or unveiling. And one of the things John does is to help his readers see Rome for what it really is. John's hope is that he will be able to dissuade his readers from associating too closely with Rome, such as becoming wealthy off their economy, and instead maintain their loyalty and faithful witness to God and the Lamb.

When the readers of Revelation, living in the first-century Roman empire, looked out at their world they saw an impressive empire, devouring more and more territory. It appeared to be as indestructible as the Titanic! They also saw the benefits of the peace and protection that this empire afforded, as well as the opportunities for prosperity and gaining wealth. But things are not as they appear. John in his vision lifts the veil so that they can see Rome in its true colors. Behind all the glamor and glitter is a godless, idolatrous, murderous, and oppressive empire, that means harm to God's kingdom and God's people. It is arrogant and usurps God's authority. In this sense, Revelation provides a thoroughgoing critique of the dominant empire of its day. In offering this John is doing the same thing as his prophetic predecessors in the Old Testament did, who railed against and exposed the dominant empires of their day, whether Egypt, Assyria, or Babylon. In fact, John draws on the language of the great prophets of Isaiah, Jeremiah, and Ezekiel to expose the dominant empire of his day: Rome. And John critiques Rome for the same sins as those previous empires: they were godless, idolatrous, oppressive, setting themselves up as God and intending harm to the people of God.

John's intention to expose Rome can be seen early on in the book.[6] In Rev 1:1–8 God is portrayed as "the one who is and who was and who is to come" (v. 4) and as the "Alpha and Omega" (v. 8). Both titles indicate God's eternity, which calls into question the claims of Rome to be "Eternal." Only God is eternal, not Rome or its gods. Furthermore, God is the "Almighty" (v. 8) and his Son, Jesus Christ, is the "ruler of the kings of the earth" (v. 5). That is, both God and the Lamb represent an authority and kingdom that stands in direct contradiction to Rome and its emperor. In contrast to the Pax Romana (Peace of Rome), the true source of "peace" comes from God. The way that God and the Lamb are presented in the first few verses of Revelation show that John offering an alternative king and kingdom to that offered by Rome. Rome's rule is illegitimate and usurps the authority of God and the Lamb. As John will show later, Rome is built on violence and bloodshed. It is built on a false system of worship of pagan gods and the emperor. It is arrogant to claim for itself what only belongs to God.

Chapters 4–5 and the throne room vision also challenges the claims of Rome to be worthy of the allegiance and worship of their subjects. The dominant image of a "throne" would directly contradict Caesar's throne. The existence of another throne would call Rome and its emperor's rule into question, by offering another kingdom and rule. Again, the throne of Caesar is illegitimate in that it attempts to usurp God's authority and claim an absolute sovereignty that belonged only to God. Rome's rule is built on violence and oppression. The first two of the seven seals in chapter 6 expose what lies behind Rome's claim to offer "Peace": warfare, violence, and bloodshed.

---

6. Much in the following paragraphs comes from Mathewson, "Social Justice in the Book of Revelation," 179–90.

> Then I heard one of the four living creatures say in a voice like thunder, "Come!" I looked, and there before me was a white horse. Its rider had a bow, and he was given a crown, and he rode out as a conqueror bent on conquest. When the Lamb opened the second seal, I heard the second living creature say, "Come!" Then another horse came out, a firey red one. Its rider was given power to take peace from the earth and to make men slay each other. To him was given a large sword (6:1–4).

Most readers take these seals as a reference exclusively to a future period of time. But if you were a Christian living in the first-century Roman Empire, you could not help but see these seals already being opened. You could not help but see correspondences with what was going on in the Roman world of your day. Specifically, in these two seals we find a picture of how Rome operated. Together they portray Rome as thirsty for conquest and expansion and wielding the sword so as to actually take peace, rather than make it! If Rome offered peace, it did so at a great cost. At the end of the day it is anything but peaceful. It was built on violence, warfare, and abusive power. In contrast, as the vision of the new Jerusalem in 21:1—22:5 show, God's throne and rule are built on justice, equity, peace, and life and well-being.

John also exposes the economic practices of Rome. The imperial Roman economy did offer the opportunity for prosperity and upward mobility, but it did so at a cost. In the third seal in 6:5–6, John sees another horse and rider, but this time the rider is carrying a scale. The scale was a symbol of economic justice. It suggests an economy out of balance. And that is exactly what this seal is about. John hears a voice that says: "A quart of wheat for a denarius, and three quarts of barely for a denarius, and do not damage the oil and the wine" (v. 6). A denarius was a typical wage for a day's work. A quart of wheat was enough to feed one person for a day, and three quarts of barely was enough to feed a family. Wheat and barley were both staples for living. The cost of living is exorbitant! But the oil and wine were not to be touched. What kind of picture is John portraying? Oil and wine were desirable for trade with Rome. It would have been profitable for provinces like Asia Minor to grow vineyards to produce oil and wine to import to Rome. However, this meant that farmers' fields which could have been used to grow the necessities of wheat and barely were used instead to produce oil and wine, which were not necessities. This resulted in a shortage of wheat and barley, especially in times of famine, so that the basic food necessities were out of reach for most because it was so exorbitantly priced. The point: John is exposing the true nature of Rome's economy—it is geared towards profitable trade and supplying Rome's thirst for items such as oil and wine. And most people in the outlying provinces, such as Asia Minor, would suffer as a result. Rome survived and flourished at the expense of the rest of the empire. Rome's economy is out of whack! John exposes the true nature of Rome's economy in order to get those churches that are compromising with Rome, and churches like Laodicea which are flourishing from Rome's economy, to have second thoughts. Are they sure they want to participate in such an economy?

The section of Revelation that probably paints Rome in its true colors more than anywhere else in the book is chapters 17 and 18. Remember Rome's claims: Goddess Roma, Eternal Rome. Rome promised peace and prosperity to all who fell under its rule. But now John says: "Do you really want to see what Rome is like? Let me show you!" Rather than a goddess, Rome is a prostitute (17:1–3), an Old Testament image of a powerful nation that exploited other nations, like Israel, economically and forced them to participate in their idolatry. Furthermore, the prostitute-Rome rides a beast, a symbol of evil, chaos, disorder, and godlessness (see Rev 13). In other words, Rome is not all it is cracked up to be. It is not as it appears. Chapter 18 then details Rome's judgment. Rather than "Eternal Rome" it is headed down the path of destruction. John uses another image to describe Rome: Babylon, an Old Testament city that was idolatrous, godless, and harmed God's people. Because Babylon/Rome has exploited other people and nations and implicated them in her unjust and idolatrous practices, because she has set herself up as God, boasting in her status, Rome's destruction and downfall will be swift and sure. Once more, she possesses a voracious appetite for expensive goods, acquired through trade, and doesn't care about the consequences on the rest of the world.

John's point in critiquing Rome is to expose its true nature, its injustice, idolatry, arrogance, and godlessness. By revealing Rome in its true colors, John is calling on the churches to distance themselves from such an empire. After all, not only Rome, but anyone participating in her idolatrous, unjust practice will go down with it. It is if John is saying, "Are you so sure now that you want to participate in Roman life, economy, and culture? Are you so sure you want to identify so closely with Rome?" Likewise, Revelation still serves to expose and critique godlessness, injustice, idolatry, arrogance, and abuse of power in our world today. The saying "If the shoe fits, wear it" applies to John's critique of Rome. Wherever we find people attempting to set up heaven on earth without God, the spirit of Rome is still alive. Revelation still calls on God's people today to resist the same idolatry, injustice, evil, and arrogant abuse of power in our nations, corporations. Where do we see it affecting our own lives today? Because one day God will destroy all such expressions of evil and all who are attached to it. This does not mean that John predicted any situation in our modern-day world, but that the same spirit or power of injustice, idolatry, oppression, and evil that was behind Babylon/Rome will continue to manifest itself until Christ comes back to destroy it. And until Christ returns, God's people must identify and avoid it at all costs.

CONCLUSION

So why did John write? What were his aims and purposes? What was God saying to his people? We misunderstand Revelation if we make it out to be a detailed prediction of the end or detailed end-times map. The book of Revelation was not meant to satisfy our curiosity of what will happen in the future. It was not meant to foster speculation about how history will end. John wrote to inspire hope in God's people of a coming new creation, to encourage obedience and holiness, to warn of complacency and compromise, to inspire worship of the one true God, and to expose and critique godless, idolatrous, exploitative, murderous empires. The way the readers today use the book of Revelation must be in line with the aims and purposes of God speaking through the author, John, for the seven churches.

PUTTING IT INTO PRACTICE

Holding onto the key of interpreting Revelation in light of the aims and purposes of God (and John's) for the book of Revelation helps us to guard against other misreadings or misuses of the book. In addition to treatment Revelation as a detailed prediction and road map to the end times, there are two common understandings of Revelation that I still frequently hear. First, "Revelation is a negative book about judgment, gloom and doom." Yes, Revelation does have visions of judgment and warfare. But these are not meant to proclaim a fatalistic message of gloom and doom. They are meant to warn people, including the churches, to repent so that they can experience the joy of salvation that God provides for his people in the new creation (21:1—22:5). God's judgments are necessary if he is to offer a world free of injustice, evil, pain, and death. He must remove anything and anyone who would oppose and attempt to destroy such a world. We live in a time where there are visible outcries for justice. God hears those cries and will one day establish a creation that is void of racial, economic, and gender injustice. But that requires that he deals with any threats and opposition to such a world. Also, the images of judgment in the seals, trumpets, and bowls should be seen as just that. They are images, not literal descriptions of the destruction that God is going to level against humanity and this world. They are images meant to evoke repentance, but also hope for those crying out for justice! The images of judgment should also not be seen as God actively sending mass destruction upon the earth and its residents. The series of seals, trumpets, and bowls should probably be seen as God allowing humanity to reap the consequences of their decision to pursue life and meaning while shoving God out of the picture. The images of judgment show humanity where such an attitude and lifestyle will lead. Again, these are not so much predictions of a future mass destruction on a global scale, as they are a call to repent in light of the certainty of God's coming judgment of sin, injustice, and evil. The main posture that God takes towards his people and towards the world is that of a slain Lamb (See Rev 5). Stemming from his holiness, justice, and his love, God sends his Son to absorb the evil of the world, to conquer death by his resurrection from the dead, and to redeem humanity to inhabit a new creation, which he graciously gives to all who love him.

A second misconception about Revelation is that the main message of John's book is that "God wins!" This is often confidently proclaimed by those who are confused by the book, and take solace that they can look beyond the debates and cling to the main purpose of the book. This view of Revelation is not so much wrong as it is incomplete. Yes, God does win in the end. But Revelation is about so much more than that. For starters, Revelation tells us that God has already won! He has already defeated sin and death, and the enemy of God and his people, Satan, through the death of the Lamb, Jesus Christ. Christ already holds the keys of death (1:18), and Satan is already a defeated foe because of Christ's death on the cross (12:10–12). God's people are already a kingdom of priests who faithfully witness to the reality of the presence of God's kingdom here and now (1:5–6). Furthermore, as this chapter has shown, Revelation's message is more than just that "God wins" in the end. Revelation was written to inspire hope in God's people in the present in light of the glorious inheritance that they have in the future, a new creation. Revelation is also meant to inspire worship, to align us to the proper center and focus of our worship, God and the Lamb, in a world of competing allegiances. It is meant to get us to follow Jesus Christ in unqualified obedience, even if it means suffering. Revelation was written to warn us of compromise and complacency, and to call us to maintain our distinctive and faithful witness. And finally, it exposes idolatry, godlessness, greed, abuse of authority, and injustice in our world today, calling us to "come out of Babylon" wherever we find it in our world today. So Revelation is so much more than the simplistic message that "God wins!" Its purpose holds a key to unlocking the messages that every Christian needs to hear today.

Key #4

AN ENIGMA,
WRAPPED IN A MYSTERY,
WRAPPED IN RIDDLE

What's this Story All about?

It is tempting when reading Revelation to get lost in the blizzard of images and symbolism, and to lose sight of the forest for the trees. In reading the last book of the Bible one feels a barrage of images constantly coming at him or her, like thick snowflakes coming down in a snow storm. The tendency sometimes is to focus exclusively on the details of the images and symbolism in each chapter and verse of Revelation, so that we lose sight of the broader picture of what is happening in the John's apocalypse. This approach often goes with the danger warned against in the last chapter. Some get so preoccupied with decoding Revelation's vision, that the reader does not step back and try to see the entire book. For these people, Revelation is a bit like a riddle that they have to figure out and solve. It is like a puzzle, and we need to assemble all the pieces in perfect fashion. For them, Revelation ends up being nothing more than a collection of predictions of the future. For others, the book of Revelation is a complete mystery, so mysterious that they can never hope to grasp it, and so they give up on trying to understand Revelation altogether. Once more, they retreat to the safer and more familiar ground of the Gospels or Paul's letters.

However, one of the keys to reading and understanding Revelation is that it tells a story,[1] it is a narrative.[2] Yes, it is unlike any other story that you are familiar with, for example, the stories of Jesus in the four Gospels. But it tells a story nevertheless. We love to hear a good story. Probably the first thing that your parents read to you as a child (if you can remember!) were story books. Stories have the power to arrest our attention, to shape us, to inspire us, to draw us into the narrative and affect us in a way that other literature can't. When Nathan the prophet confronted David concerning his sin with Bathsheba, Nathan told him a story that actually got David to condemn himself (2 Sam 12:1–7). When Jesus wanted to drive home his point about the kingdom of God, he told short stories known as parables (see Matt 13 for example). Revelation is also a story. It is a narrative—a narration of a vision that John had.

One of the key principles for interpretation of any piece of literature, especially narrative or story, is that meaning is dependent on the literary context of any passage. A reader of the book of 1 Corinthians cannot understand chapter 9 of Paul's book without putting it within the broader context of the issue of eating meat offered to idols that Paul addresses in chapters 8 to 10, and the larger issues related to social elitism and disunity throughout the entire book. Paul appeals to his giving up his rights to receive financial support, although he had a right to it as an apostle, as an example for the Corinthian believers who should give up their right to eat meat offered to idols for the sake of the greater good of the body of Christ. The reader of the Sermon on the Mount in Matt 5–7 must see how it fits within the overall context of Jesus's teaching on the arrival of the kingdom of God and how he has come to fulfill the story of the Old Testament. The same is true with Revelation. We need to have a sense of the story told in the last book of the Bible. Revelation tells a story; in a sense it is a drama, and we need a sense of the whole in order to better understand each part. You would not go on Netflix, find a series to watch, choose an episode in Season 3, fast forward through part of it and watch 5 minutes, turn it off, and then try to make sense of it. No. You have to watch the entire sequence, from beginning to end, to make sense of it. The same is true of the book of Revelation. One of the first things that the reader of Revelation should do is sit down and read the entire book from beginning to end, without trying to figure out and decipher every last detail. This will give a sense of the story that Revelation is telling. One of my favorite Western authors is Louis L'Amour. Whenever I

---

1. By using the word "story" to refer to the book of Revelation, or even the Gospels, I am not suggesting they are fictional or unreal, but that they communicate truth through the form of a story or narrative.

2. Ressiguie, *Revelation of John*.

read one of his novels I feel that I can visualize the scenes and the characters, and the story draws me in and I feel that I am there experiencing all the sights, the sounds, the tension, and the ups and downs of the story. That is what we need to do with Revelation—allow it to draw us in so that we experience the sights and sounds of the book, the joy and even terror of its scenes, the tension and resolution. So what is the story that Revelation tells?

THE STORY OF THE SEVEN CHURCHES

We have already seen in the previous chapter that the book of Revelation is the story of the seven historical churches in Asia Minor, and their struggle to live out their faithful witness in the Roman world (chs. 2–3), a world dominated by Rome's religions and politics. It is a story of churches that are suffering abuse at the hands of the empire, but even more so churches that are tempted to compromise and become complacent. The book of Revelation is addressed to them. But their story also is reflected in the larger vision in chs. 4–22 (see ch. 3 above). However, the narrative in 4–22 tells its own story, which is meant to help the churches in 2–3 makes sense of their own stories. Revelation situates the story of the seven churches in a specific geographical location (the Roman province of Asia Minor) and at a specific time in history (end of the first century AD under Roman rule) in chapters 2 to 3. However, Revelation also places the churches' situation against the backdrop of a larger story found in chapters 4 to 22. As we will soon see, the story in 4–22 contains other actors besides the seven churches in 2–3, such as angels, Satan, the nations, God, and the Lamb. It spans a period of time that reaches back long before the time of the churches and forward to the future when God will bring history to its close and establish his worldwide kingdom. It also encompasses a geographical area larger than Asia Minor, embracing the entire earth, but also the heavenly realms. That is, Revelation takes the situation and story of the churches in 2–3 and situates them on a larger map temporally and geographically.

I live in Denver, Colorado, and I often find myself consulting Google Maps to find a specific store I need to visit. When I google the store name, a map comes up that shows a "zoomed-in" view of the street on which the store is located. But I always find the need to see how that location relates to other landmarks in the city and other streets, such as I-25, the major artery that goes through Denver, and how it relates to my location in Littleton. So I zoom back out to see the larger map and to locate the store I am looking for in relationship to the larger layout of the city of Denver and other major landmarks in addition to my own home. This helps me to see where it is in relationship to these other features. It gives me a sense of how long it is going to take, and which route I will travel. This explains a little what is going on in Revelation. In chapters 2 to 3 John zooms in on the seven churches, their specific locations in Asia Minor, a specific point on the historical map, and their specific time period (probably at the end of the first century). Then in chapters 4 to 22 he zooms out to see the broader map, the larger landscape of the entire world, the nations, the heavenly world, God, the Lamb, angels, and the dragon, Satan. And he sees the larger span of time, going back even to creation (Gen 1–3) and forward to the end-time new creation (Rev 21:1—22:5). He does not abandon the seven churches and their location, but merely expands and broadens their world. This enables John and his readers to see their situation in a brand new light, and to gain a new perspective on where they are on the map. Chapters 4 to 22, then, is a narrative in and of itself, with characters, a story line, a plot, tension, and resolution. But what is the story all about? Let's start by introducing the main characters in the vision of Rev 4–22.

THE STORY OF REVELATION 4–22

The Main Actors

Any good story, movie, or novel will have one or more main characters and will introduce those characters at some point, usually near the beginning, and perhaps reveal something of their character. Usually in such stories there are major and minor characters, and good and bad ones. The same is true with the story of Rev 4–22. Revelation is a story with main characters, both good and evil, which act out the story. Let's introduce the cast of main characters in Revelation's story.[3]

God

God is depicted primarily as the sovereign creator of all things and the ruler of the entire universe. In chapter 4 his status as sovereign ruler is indicated by the image of the throne upon which he sits, a symbol of sovereignty. There he is also worshiped as sovereign ruler and creator of all that exists (vv. 9–11). He is the holy and eternal God who stands at the beginning and end of all history, as its origin and its goal. Sometimes the main characters are revealed through names and titles given to them. An important title for

---

3. Mathewson, *Companion to the Book of Revelation*, 20–23.

God is "the one who is, who was, and who is coming" (1:4, 8; 4:8) which draws on Exod 3:14 ("I am who I am"). He is the "alpha and the omega, the beginning and end" (1:8; 21:6). God is eternally existent, stands at the beginning and end of history, and is also coming to consummate his redemptive plan and purposes for his people and for all creation.[4] It is God's sovereign rule, which is realized in heaven (ch. 4), that is contested by the affairs of this earth. God is also the ultimate source of the vision that is given to John (1:1). God also is and represents truth and justice (6:10; 15:3; 16:7; 19:2, 9).

The Lamb

The Lamb is God's primary agent for accomplishing his redemptive purposes and establishing his kingdom on earth. It is as the slain Lamb that Jesus accomplishes God's redemptive purposes for all creation, indicated by his taking the scroll in Rev 5. His death purchases a people from all the nations and peoples of the earth (1:5–6; see below). As the slain Lamb Jesus also serves as a model for suffering witness for his followers. Jesus is God's Messiah, in fulfillment of Old Testament promises of a coming royal king from the tribe of Judah (5:6), but he will overcome by his suffering death. Yet another common image of Jesus is as the future coming judge. The Lamb is God's agent of judgment on the whole world (19:11–21). The Lamb is closely identified with (as!) God, in that he shares God's throne (5:13), receives the same worship (5:11–12), and shares the same title of eternity: he is "the alpha and the omega, the first and the last, the beginning and the end"; 22:13; see 1:17). He is the ultimate faithful and true witness (3:14; 19:11).

Angels

Angels also play a key role in John's apocalyptic story. They function as agents and servants of God and the Lamb in a number of roles. They (including the twenty-four elders and four living creatures) testify in heaven to God's sovereignty and rule (Rev 4–5; 7:11–12). In this sense, they represent what must take place in all creation, not just in heaven. Angelic beings also serve to mediate the vision to John, and sometimes interact with John (7:13–14; 19:9–10; 22:6, 8–11), and even guide him in major visionary moments: the vision of Babylon (ch. 17) and the vision of the new Jerusalem (ch. 21:9—22:5). They also form an army which is responsible for the defeat

---

4. Bauckham, *Theology of Revelation*, 25–30.

of Satan and his angels and proclaim important messages about the coming of God's kingdom to earth (14:6–11). All in all, they support the agenda of God and the Lamb, and the activity of the people of God.

The People of God

The people of God are God's primary agents on earth in witnessing to the reality of God's sovereign reign, the Lamb, God's Messiah, and the truth of the gospel and God's kingdom on earth. They are identified as those who have been redeemed (by the Lamb) from every tribe, tongue, nation, and people. They are a kingdom of priests unto God, who represent his presence and rule in the world (5:9–10). That is, they are a universal, trans-cultural people in their makeup. They follow the Lamb wherever he goes in their life on this earth (14:4). There are a number of metaphors that probably all refer to the people of God as a whole: the 144,000 thousand, the innumerable multitude, and the two witnesses (ch. 11), the bride of the Lamb (19:7–8; 21:2, 9), and the end-time new Jerusalem (21:1—22:5). All of these express something about the relationship of the people of God to God and the Lamb and their role in the story.

Dragon

The primary antagonist (the main "bad guy") in the story, and the root source of all opposition to God, the Lamb, the people of God, and God's intention to establish his kingly reign on earth is the dragon, Satan. In a sense, the story of 4–22 could be described as God vs. Satan. This antagonist has a long history that takes the story of Revelation all the way back to creation in Gen 1–3. Twice, the dragon is clearly identified as the serpent of old from the first creation account in the book of Genesis (12:9; 20:2). The author develops this character so that you can't miss his true nature. The identity of the dragon as the deceiver of the whole world (12:9; 20:3, 10) reflects his role of deceiving the first human beings, Adam and Eve, to sin against God. In fact, John can hardly mention the dragon without mentioning deception! He now continues his deceiving activity and opposition to God and his people in the current story of Rev 4–22. As the deceiver Satan clearly contrasts with God who is faithful and true (see above). Satan is the one who not only deceives, but who persecutes and accuses the people of God (12:10).

Two Beasts

In the same way that God has his agents in the Lamb, the Messiah, and in the people of God (and the angels), the dragon, Satan, also has his agents through which he accomplishes his nefarious purposes in the world. They are two hideous looking beasts (11:7; 13), Beast 1 and Beast 2, who look a lot like the dragon himself. The first beast has horns and seven heads (13:1), and the second beast has horns and speaks like a dragon (13:11) This is what we would expect since they share his character and evil intentions. The dragon inspires and delegates his authority to the two beasts, and the first beast commands universal worship. The dragon and his two beastly offspring form an "unholy trinity."

Demons

The demons also stand with the dragon and the two beasts. In fact, they have their home and origin in the same place: the bottomless pit (9, 11, 20). The fact that the locusts in 9:2–3 come from the abyss suggests they symbolize demons. They are part of the dragon, Satan's, army (9:1; 12:7–9). Three frogs in 16:13 are identified as three evil spirits that come from the dragon and two beasts. They aid the dragon and the beasts in carrying out their evil intentions in the world. They harm humanity as part of the plagues poured out on the world (16:13), and they ultimately lie behind the idols that humanity is tempted to worship (9:20).

Kings of the Earth, Nations, Earth Dwellers

A large group that plays an important role in Revelation's story is the people from the nations that appear in numerous places throughout John's story. For the most part, the people from the earth, or the nations, play an *ambiguous* role in Revelation. First, for much of the book they are in a league with the dragon and the beasts. They are deceived by the dragon, Satan, to follow him, and his beastly cohort. They persecute the people of God (6:9; 11) and give their allegiance to the beast. They constitute an army in submission to their ruler (16:16; 20:8) and are subject to the final judgment (ch. 19). However, the nations also end up in the end time new Jerusalem (21:24, 26), apparently the same group that previously submitted to the beast and gave allegiance to the dragon.

These are the major players in the drama of Revelation's story. As you can see Revelation has its protagonists and antagonists, and the above characters are described and developed at some length (except for maybe the angels and demons, but their character is not in doubt), like the main characters in a movie or novel. Now that the stage is set, let's look at the story itself.

Revelation's Story

Like a good story, Revelation has an introduction, and a middle, and an end. It has a plot! It describes scenes in vivid detail as the main actors play out there roles. It plays on the senses of the reader: sight, sound, taste (a bitter and sweet scroll), even smell (smoke and sulphur!). It draws the reader into its story to experience what John saw and experienced in his vision. The story contained in Revelation's main vision (4:1—22:5) begins with a heavenly scene where all of heaven acknowledges God's sovereignty and worship him as the ruler and creator of all (ch. 4). The Lamb is also worshiped in heaven because he is the exclusive means by which God accomplishes his redemptive purposes in the world (ch. 5). God is worshiped because he is the creator of all, and the Lamb is worshiped because he is the redeemer of all. Stop and read chapters 4 to 5 in one sitting, and let the images roll before your eyes and impact you. You come away with the impression that heaven is a place of order, perfect harmony, beauty, and serenity. Heaven is ordered with the throne of God situated at its very center, and all of heaven arranged in concentric circles around it, offering ceaseless praise in harmonious worship. Colors dance across the page in brilliant display as John describes the heavenly environs. The sea, often a sign of chaos and foreboding later in the book (13:1; 20:13; 21:1), is calm and serene here (4:6).

In this opening vision the reader is introduced to the main cast of characters in the story: God (the One seated on the throne), the Lamb, and the angels, who worship God and the Lamb and represent all creation.[5] Besides introducing us to the main cast of characters, the opening of the vision with the heavenly scene serves a twofold purpose: 1) It contrasts with the scenes of chaos and disharmony on the earth in the rest of the vision. It is a comfort to the reader, ancient and modern, to know that God is sovereignly on his throne, his will is being accomplished, and all is calm and in order, no matter how chaotic things appear on this present earth; but there is a more important reason for this opening. 2) After reading this opening scene of the story, the reader cannot help but ask the question: How will this scene in heaven become a reality on earth? How will God's will and sovereignty that are perfectly realized in heaven become a reality on an earth full of

5. deSilva, *Discovering Revelation*, 95.

chaos and evil, where God's will is contested and rejected? How can the world become a place of order, peace, and harmony, a place where God and the Lamb are worshiped as the center of all things? The rest of the story of Revelation answers just these questions. This is already hinted at with the image of the "scroll" in God's right hand in 5:1. The scroll symbolizes God's plan for redeeming the entire world, for establishing his rule and presence throughout all creation. The slain Lamb is the means by which God will accomplish his purposes in the world. The rest of Revelation will tell this story.

This is where we need to shift our attention for a moment to the earthly scenes in Revelation. And this is where the antagonists (the bad guys!) come in. As already noted, this world contests God's will and rule. This world is under the dominion of the dragon, Satan, and his two beastly cohorts (chs. 12–13). The kingdoms of this world belong to Satan and his minions. He is the ruler of this world (see Eph 2:2) in clear opposition to the picture of God seated on his throne in chapter 4. The author of the story of Revelation (in the form of a recorded vision) takes the reader all the way back to the first creation and the entrance of sin into the world when the dragon, Satan, deceived the first people. This is clear in the way the dragon is identified, as "the serpent of old", and the deceiver (12:9; 20:1–3; see Gen 3:1). From the time the serpent deceived humanity and set his nefarious plan into motion, the world has been under the rule of the dragon; his throne has been at the center of creation (which is manifested locally in places like Pergamum). And the dragon continues his deceptive activity in John's story (12:9; 20:8).

The two beasts in chapter 13 are the earthly agents of Satan's evil and anti-godly activity in this world in that, in contrast to the scene in heaven, they try to establish worldwide worship of the dragon and acknowledgement of his reign. As some students of Revelation have recognized, the dragon and the two beasts constitute sort of an "unholy Trinity" which contrasts with God, the Lamb, and the Spirit (see Rev 1:4–6), further highlighting their antagonistic role. Their goal is to destroy God's kingdom and the world over which they oppressively reign and to deceive humanity from worshiping the true God and the Lamb. The demons play a further role in bringing pain, evil, and disorder to the present creation. In contrast to the four living creatures in chapter 4, whose hybrid makeup represent order and harmony,[6] the locusts in Rev 9:1–12, which symbolize demonic beings (they come out of the abyss, the home of demons), are a grotesque and hideous combination of animal and human parts that represent disorder, chaos, and horror: heads like humans, golden crowns, hair like a woman, teeth like a

---

6. Resseguie, *Revelation of John*, 112.

lion, breastplates of iron, tails like a scorpion.[7] Such is Satan's influence on the present world.

The role of the antagonists in the story is clear: they oppose God and the Lamb, and the establishment of their good, just, righteous, and loving rule on earth. And they oppose and persecute God's people. They attempt to secure their own hold over this creation and its inhabitants, and they enforce it through deception and oppression. They are out to destroy the world, and anyone who sides with God and the Lamb.

At the center of the conflict between God and the Lamb and the forces of evil stands the nations and people of the earth. They are presented as under the sway of the dragon and beasts' reign over the earth. They are described in various ways: the nations of the earth, rulers and kings of the earth, the earth dwellers. They are the subjects of the dragon's deceptive activity (just as were Adam and Eve) and give worship and allegiance to the dragon and beasts. They acknowledge and even marvel at the power and authority of the dragon and his beastly cohorts (they are more than just allies since they are his very offspring). They also persecute and put to death the people of God. The main point is that they have given their allegiances to the dragon and the beasts because they have been deceived into doing so. The same deceptive activity that lured Adam and Eve to rebel against God and go their own way is now present in the world of the story of Revelation. The question that this raises is: How will God reverse this state of affairs? How will God's will and sovereignty, perfectly acknowledged in heaven, come to an earth that contradicts it, and how is God going to rescue that nations from the deceptive rule of Satan to be part of his kingdom and rule, and to worship and acknowledge his sovereignty, as heaven does in chapters 4 to 5? How will God transfer the nations from under the oppressive rule of the dragon to loyalty and allegiance to the God who created all things and who rules from heaven? Again, the rest of the book of Revelation will answer this question.

First, God will establish his rule on earth through both judgment and redemption. God has already acted to bring redemption, to redeem people from the oppressive rule of Satan and the beasts, through the death of Jesus Christ, the Lamb. He has already defeated and unseated Satan (12:7–11). Satan's doom has already been sealed, though he is allowed a brief time to wreak havoc (12:12: "he has great wrath, because he knows he has a short time"), and only with permission. In a previous chapter we referred to a common misconception of Revelation: it is only about how God wins! But we responded by saying that Revelation is about how God has already won!

7. Koester, *Revelation and the End of All Things*, 102.

He has already defeated death and Satan. He has already provided redemption and salvation through the sacrificial, slain Lamb. Furthermore, God is already in the process of judging this world. After the heavenly scene in chapters 4 to 5, much of Revelation can be seen as revolving around three sets of seven judgments: the seals (ch. 6), the trumpets (chs. 8–9), and the bowls (ch. 16). Each of these three sets of judgments are increasingly intense judgments by God on this present earth. The number "seven" in each case is intentional: it suggests not necessarily seven literal, precise judgments that will happen in that order, but as the number seven does elsewhere, they symbolize the complete and perfect judgments of God. Notice that each set is increasingly intense and severe. The seals affect one-fourth, the trumpets one-half, and there is no limitation on the effects of the bowls. The point is not to set out a precise chronological sequence of judgments, but to say something about the certainty and nature of God's judgment in this world. God is already judging the earthly systems (political, economic, religious) and the things that are under the sway of Satan and have been corrupted by him. And these judgments will become increasingly intense. If these judgment scenes shout to the world, the shout gets louder and louder with each series. They seem to represent God "undoing" this present creation, exposing it for what it really is and showing its true character under the rule of the dragon. In a sense God is "uncreating" the world to make room for a new creation (but we are getting ahead of ourselves!). The increasing intensity of the judgments anticipates the final judgment that is coming in chapters 19 to 20. They are "warning shots" of a greater judgment still to come when Christ returns to earth. Therefore, not only are they true judgments on this present world, as God is in the process of transferring the world form under the sovereignty of Satan to being under his rule, but they also call on people to repent in order to avoid the final, coming judgment that they warn about. At the end of the trumpet judgments and at the bowl judgments John says that people "still did not repent" (9:20) or "refused to repent and glorify his name" (16:9). Yes, these are judgments, but the hope is that humanity would respond by repenting and turning to worship the one true God, even if they refuse to do so.

Then comes the ultimate judgments in chapters 19 to 20. In these final chapters the reader finds a series of "removal" or judgment scenes. Everything that stands in the way of the establishment of God's holy, just, and righteous kingdom and his peoples' enjoyment of it, is removed in judgment. First Babylon is removed in judgment (ch. 18), then the nations are judged in the final battle (19:11–21). Then the three primary antagonists are removed in the reverse order in which they were introduced in chapters 12 to 13. First the two beasts are judged and thrown into the lake of fire

(19:20), then Satan is judged and joins his beastly cohorts in the lake of fire (20:10). Finally, there is a general "clean-up" scene where everything is removed in judgment, including the present creation (20:11–15) which was wrecked by evil, injustice, and the place where Satan ruled. All barriers have been removed. All that remains is the establishment of God's new creation (21:1—22:5).

Second, here is where another main character in John's story emerges that serves to fulfill God's purposes of establishing his reign and rule on earth, and the acknowledgment of his sovereignty through praise and worship: *the people of God.* The people of God are those whom the Lamb has redeemed through his death from every tribe, people, language, and nation (1:5–6; 5:9). They make up the transcultural people of God that function as a kingdom of priests who reign on the earth. The fact that they are a kingdom of priests suggests that they are a visible indication of a counter rule to the dragon and the beasts. They represent another kingdom and another allegiance. Overall, their primary role is *to witness* to the reality of God, the Lamb, and their kingdom on earth. But chapters 6 to 20 are characterized by the conflict between not only God and Satan, but the people of God on earth and the beasts.[8] The people of God are to witness to the truth in the face of a world that contests and contradicts them, a world under the deceptive grip of the dragon's reign. This means opposition and hostility towards the people of God, in the form of persecution and even death. It is through their witness that the nations see an alternative kingdom and are confronted with the reality of the heavenly scene in chapters 4 to 5 on earth. Through their allegiance to God and the Lamb, even in the face of suffering at the hands of a hostile world, the people of God as a kingdom of priests witness to the reality of what takes place in heaven, and what God intends to accomplish on this earth (see Rev 21:1—22:5). They model the life of the new creation in the present. And their faithful witness is part of winning the nations from allegiance to the dragon and beasts to God and the Lamb.

The story ends with the heavenly scene in chapters 4 to 5 finally become a reality on earth in 21:1—22:5. The reader finally hears the words: "And I saw a new heaven and a new earth" (21:1). The attentive reader cannot help but hear an echo of Gen 1:1: "In the beginning God created the heavens and the earth." That creation, marred by sin and under the dominion of the dragon and beasts, is now replaced with a new one. The throne of God and the Lamb in heaven (chs. 4–5) is now situated on a renewed earth (22:1, 3). The earth is no longer under the rule and authority of the dragon and two beasts, but now is under the rule of God and the Lamb, with his

8. Bauckham, *Theology of Revelation,* 150.

people ruling alongside of them (22:5). The faithful witness of the people of God and the judgments of God that have eventually removed all evil and opposition to God's reign has given way to the establishment of God's kingdom on earth. In contrast to the scenes of chaos, disorder, disharmony, and evil, the new creation is a place of beauty, harmony, order, peace, and holiness. In contrast to sin and death there is unending righteousness and life! The bride-new Jerusalem (21:2, 9) has replaced the prostitute-Babylon (chs. 17–18). The nations that formerly gave their allegiance to the dragon and beasts, now give their allegiance to God and the Lamb. The nations walk by the light given off by the new Jerusalem, and the glory of the kings and nations will be brought into the new city (21:24, 26). The transfer of the kingdoms of this earth from Satan and the beasts to God and the Lamb is also accompanied by the transfer of allegiance of the people who belong to the world. They join the redeemed and experience life in the new creation. They now recognize the sovereignty and holiness of the One seated on the throne, who is now at the center of the new creation.

This is the story of Revelation in a nutshell. It is about how the heavenly scene in chapters 4 to 5 finally becomes a reality on earth in chapters 21 to 22. In this sense, chapters 4 to 5 and 21 to 22 are bookends. As British New Testament scholar, Richard Bauckham, proposed, Revelation could be seen as sort of an extended commentary on part of the Lord's prayer from Matt 6:9–10:[9] "Our Father who is in heaven . . . your kingdom come, your will be done, on earth as it is in heaven." This is a prayer for God's rule, will, and sovereignty, which is already realized in heaven, to one day become a reality on earth. This corresponds to the story of Revelation. Chapters 4 to 5 is the part of the Lord's prayer that confesses "your will be done . . . as it is in heaven." Then chapters 21 to 22 and the new creation vision correspond to and are the answer to the part of the Lord's prayer that says, "your will be done on earth." Revelation is the story of how God's will done in heaven (chs. 4–5) is finally done on earth (chs. 21–22). Everything in between these two sections is how God accomplishes this: through the sacrificial death of the Lamb on the cross, to redeem a people for himself, through the faithful witness of those people to the reality of God and the Lamb's kingdom on earth, even in the face of suffering and death, through the defeat of Satan already by the Lamb's death and resurrection, through the judgments already poured out on this earth to "undo" the world and its systems, and through rescuing the nations from the oppressive and deceptive sway of the Dragon and beasts to worship the one true God and the Lamb. Then the final judgment, and then the newly created heavens and earth!

9. For this suggestion see Bauckham, *Theology of Revelation*, 40.

Consistent with the Lord's prayer that God's kingdom in heaven comes to earth, the prayers of the saints also play a key role in Revelation in the establishment of God's kingdom on earth. In 5:9 the four living creatures hold golden bowls full of incense, which John identifies as the prayers of the saints. In the fifth seal John sees a vision of the souls under the altar who cry out to God for vengeance: "How long sovereign Lord, holy and true, until you judge the inhabitants of the earth and avenge our blood?" (6:10). In one sense, the rest of the book, including the establishment of the new creation (21:1—22:5), can all be seen as a response to this cry or prayer. Again, in chapter 8 before the blowing of the seven trumpet plagues an angel holds a censer full of incense, which is identified as the prayers of the saints (8:3). These references suggest that the establishment of God's kingdom, even through the judgments, comes in response to the prayers of the people of God. This is the overall story that John's vision tells. It is not just a collection of predictions of the end, or end-time prophesies. It tells a carefully constructed and unfolding story of God's purposes in this world through the sacrifice of the Lamb and through the faithful witness of his people to reclaim the world and its people from the rule and power of Satan and his cohorts to serve and worship the true God in a new creation where God's sovereignty and holiness are perfectly realized by all, and where God's will is done on earth, as it is in heaven! And so the story of Revelation ends!

In the previous chapter of this book we saw that Revelation is a story about the seven historical churches in chapters 2 to 3. The book of Revelation, like any other book in the New Testament, is meant to be understood in its historical context. The context of Revelation is seven churches attempting to live out their faithful witness in the context of the first-century Roman Empire. That is, Revelation is located in a specific geographical area at a specific point in time in history. But in this chapter we saw that the story of Revelation is much broader than the story of the seven churches existing in the shadow of first-century imperial Rome. The story reaches up to heaven, it reaches back to the birth of Christ and even to the first creation, and it reaches forward to the wrap-up of God's redemptive purposes in Christ at his second coming. Where do we find the seven churches in this story? Earlier, I compared the seven churches and their situation to Google Maps, which looks at a specific street and city block. However, chapters 4 to 22 zoom out to a larger map which includes a larger perspective, including the past, the future, and heaven itself. Revelation situates the seven churches and their stories as part of this larger story of the conflict between God and Satan, and God's plan to establish his kingdom on earth and bring his redemptive plan to its culmination. He does this through the sacrifice of the

Lamb, through preliminary judgments, calling for repentance, and through the faithful witness of the people of God.

The churches in Rev 2–3 are the current manifestation of this story in a specific time and location. They are to see themselves as they relate to this broader narrative, and to adjust their perspective and respond appropriately. They are the current people of God, under the rule of God and called to worship God and carry out their faithful witness. The conflict between God and his people and Satan and his beastly cohorts is currently manifested in the conflict between the seven churches and the pagan Roman Empire. The new creation stands as a motivation for them to persevere in their present circumstances. The vision of Revelation in 4–22 helps the churches to see their place within the larger story that goes back to creation and forward to the new creation, and upward to include heaven. This story, then, enables them to see the true nature of their conflict, what it means to overcome and to be faithful witnesses in their context, and the reward of their life and existence in the new creation for persevering. Overall, it provides the motivation for faithfulness, worship of the true God, and unqualified obedience to God and the Lamb, no matter what they face.

How John Tells His Story

In one sense, the story of Revelation has a beginning, middle, and end. It moves in an overall straightforward manner, from beginning to end. On the other hand, the careful reader will notice that Revelation is not simply a simple, forward-moving story, like one might find in a historical biography, for example (although these do not always move in a straightforward manner from beginning to end). Revelation's story could also be seen as cyclical in nature. That is, Revelation begins with the present, or even past, and moves to the future wrap-up of history at the coming of Christ to fulfill his promises, only to start the cycle again, and again. For example, at the end of the seal sequence in chapter 6, John ends with a clear reference to the final judgment at the end of history, with the reference to the Day of the Lamb's wrath.

> And there was a great earthquake, and the sun became as black as sackcloth, and the whole moon became as blood. And the stars of heaven fell upon the earth, as a fig tree throws off its figs when shaken by a strong wind, and heaven disappeared as a scroll rolled up, and every mountain and island was removed from their place. And the kings of the earth and the magistrates and the high ranking officers and the rich and the strong and

> the slave and free hid themselves in the caves and the rocks in
> the mountains and they said to the mountains and to the rocks,
> "Fall on us and hide us from the face of the one seated on the
> throne and from the wrath of the Lamb. For the great day of
> their wrath has come, and who is able to stand?" (6:12–17)

Here the reader is clearly standing at the end-time judgment at what theologians call the Second Coming of Christ. Yet we still have sixteen chapters left to go in Revelation! In the very next chapter (ch. 7) the author has a vision of the 144,000 on earth, who go out and conquer through their faithful witness, then the vision shifts to a "heavenly" scene of the people of God portrayed as an innumerable multitude standing victorious in God's presence. The rest of chapter 7, with its reference to serving God day and night (v. 15), never hungering or thirsting (v. 16), no sun (v. 16), the Lamb's throne at the center and leading his people to springs of water (v. 17), and God wiping the tears from his people's eyes (v. 17), recalls features of the new creation in 21:1—22:5 and suggests that we are once again at the end of history, the fulfillment of God's redemptive purposes in the future with the rewarding of his faithful people of God in a new creation. Yet we still have fifteen more chapters to go in Revelation.

In chapter 11 the author begins in the present with the faithful witness of the church, symbolized by the two witnesses. They are put to death by the beast and apparently defeated. Yet God raises them up, a reference to the final resurrection at the coming of Christ (see 1 Cor 15). Then the seventh trumpet (which was delayed after the first six in chapters 8 to 9) is finally blown and a hymn divulges what happens at the sound of the seventh trumpet:

> The kingdom of the world has become the kingdom of our Lord
> and his Christ, and he will reign for ever and ever (v. 15)

Then another hymn, this time sung by the twenty-four elders (see Rev 4), further reveals:

> We give thanks to you, Lord God Almighty, the One who is and
> who was, because you have taken your great power and have be-
> gun to reign. The nations were angry and your wrath has come.
> The time has come for judging the dead, and for rewarding your
> servants the prophets, and your saints and those who reverence
> your name, both small and great—and for destroying those who
> destroy the earth. (vv. 17–18)

Both of these hymns show that we have reached the end, the establishment of God's kingdom, the pouring out of God's wrath in end-time judgment, the judging of the dead (see 20:11–15) and the final reward of the saints. Yet we still have not reached the end of the book. In chapter 12 John takes us all the way back to the birth of Christ, with the reference to the birth of a son (v. 5–6), and even further back to the first creation in Gen 1–3, with a reference to the serpent of old in 12:9. Then chapter 14 contains alternating visions of final judgment and final salvation of the major characters in chapters 12 to 13: the saints, and those who received the mark of the beast. But we still have eight chapters to go. The end is finally reached in chapters 19 to 22. In chapters 19 to 20 we find a full-blown picture of end time judgment, where everything is removed which is a threat to the people of God, God's kingdom, and the enjoyment of the saints' inheritance. Then once everything is removed in judgment by the end of chapter 20, chapters 21 to 22 give a full-blown picture of end-time salvation in the form of the new creation, with God and the Lamb living in the midst of their people.

How do we make sense of this? First, these starts and stops cover the same ground: they start with the present and sometimes the past, then move to the future, the coming of Christ to establish God's end-time kingdom. The reason for this is that John is providing different perspectives on the same time and events. John uses different images and pictures to describe the past, present, and future so that we see the world and our situation from fresh perspectives, and so that we get the point. Therefore, in chapter 7 John describes the people of God in the present as an army, 144,000 strong, who go out to do battle and overcome. But then he sees them as a numberless multitude standing in God's presence victorious, waving palm branches and experiencing life in the new creation. But in chapter 11 he covers the same ground again but with a different set of images. This time he sees the people of God as two faithful witness, who are overcome (apparently) by the beast. But then God raises them and vindicates them at the future coming of Christ to bring God's kingdom. Again, both visions cover the same territory and interpret the situation of the church from different perspectives using different images. Chapters 12 to 13 cover the same ground as chapters 7 and 11, but now using different images, the dragon and two beasts, the mark of the beast, and they take the reader back in time to the death of Christ and even to the first creation where the serpent of old deceived the first people (12:9). It is as if John is saying, "Let me tell you the story of the people of God and their role in the world and show you where it is all headed. Now let me tell you the same story again, this time using different images. And now let me tell you the story again, to show you a different perspective on things." It is a bit like strolling through an art gallery and seeing different artistic depictions. Each provides a different picture of reality, with different colors, hues, and images.

Second, the brief visions of judgment and salvation earlier in the book are meant to whet our appetite for and anticipate a fuller picture of final judgment and salvation . . . and the reader is scarcely disappointed. All of the initial visions are preliminary, incomplete, leaving the reader begging for more details. And that is what we find in chapters 19 to 22: all the stops are pulled out as God reveals the final wrap-up of his redemptive purposes with a final and full visions of judgment (19–20) and salvation (21–22). This will happen when Christ returns to consummate God's purposes on earth. Perhaps the expectation and anticipation in reading Revelation should create a corresponding expectation and anticipation in the people of God as they live their lives in the world and experience the tension of faithful witness in a hostile world while waiting for the intervention of God to bring his redemptive plan to its end-time goal.

Another important feature of John's story to pay attention to is the repetition of the words "I saw," or "After these things, I saw." To be fair, there are an equal number of references to what John "heard" throughout Revelation. These words literally occur all throughout John's vision, and makes it clear that John is describing what he saw (and heard) in a vision he received. But should we go further? Is John telling us more? Some have suggested that John is telling us the order in which these events will take place. The repeated "I saw" corresponds to the order in which the events in John's vision will take place. But we have already seen that John's story does not always easily move in a strict chronological fashion. Chapters 6 and 7 contain visions of end-time judgment (sixth seal) and salvation (7:7–11). But then chapter 12 takes us all the way back to the birth of Christ and even earlier (the first creation). So how should we treat the "I saw" or "after these things I saw" or "I heard" throughout Revelation? These words tell us the order in which John *saw* or *heard* things, not necessarily the order in which they will occur (or did occur). That is, John is saying "I saw . . . . Then after that, here is what I saw next . . . . Then here is what I saw next." He is not telling us the order in which they occur or will occur in history, but he is simply relating the order in which he saw the visions. For example, in chapters 19 to 22 we find John's grand finale of end-time judgment and salvation. It is peppered with the words "I saw."

However, while there is a general chronology, in that the time of the churches witness and conflict with the beast and initial judgments (6–18) precede the end time judgments in Rev 19–20, and the end-time judgment and removal (19–20) probably precede salvation and renewal (21–22), within that John is not trying to provide a detailed chronology giving the curious reader details as to the exact order of end-time events. Instead, he is more interested in giving a series of visions that tell us sometime about the certainty and character of the end-time judgment and salvation in order to motivate God's people to holy living. More importantly, they give us insight into the character of God, a God who is holy, loving, and just—another indication that we cannot use Revelation to construct end-time charts to discover exactly how and in what order things will transpire in the future and where our time might fall within this scheme. Revelation is simply not interested in giving the reader that kind of information.

NOW THAT THE STORY IS OVER . . . .

After the lengthy vision in 4:1—22:5, there is still a major part of the last chapter left to go. Now that John is finished recording his vision, he now returns to the "real world" of his readers. When you go to a movie theatre you enter the theatre and immerse yourself in the movie, its world, its characters, its plot. You often forget what is going on outside, and what happened earlier that day (maybe you had a bad day at work!). But when the movie is over you exit the theatre and re-enter the "real world" of everyday life. In 22:6–22 the readers in a sense exit the theatre of John's vision and re-enter their real world. But they are not leaving a fantasy or fictional world and now coming back to a real world; instead, they have seen their own world portrayed in a new light, in light of the story in 4–22, and are now to "re-enter" or better "re-engage" their specific world in a new way. Rev 22:6–22 is meant to provide instructions on how they are to apply and live out the vision that they just entered and experienced in 4:1—22:5. These verses provide "reading instructions" or better, "living instructions" for the readers to guide them in responding to and living out the vision in their specific location and time. It begins with a reminder of the gravity of the words that they have just read (22:6). It reminds the readers of the true object of worship (22:6–9), of who Jesus is (22:12, 16), of his soon return to consummate God's plan (22:7, 12, 20), and they call for unqualified obedience to God and the Lamb (22:7, 12, 14, 17, 18–19).[10] In this sense the story of Revelation is not over. The next scene in the drama of Revelation's story is written by the people of God who follow the instructions in 2:6–21 and put them into practice.

PUTTING IT INTO PRACTICE

What does this story mean for the reader of Revelation? For many Christians, Revelation is little more than a repository of end-time predictions,

10. Mathewson, *Companion to the Book of Revelation*, 129–32.

which can be extracted to construct a nice, neat chart or timeline of how the future events will unfold. However, the way that Revelation tells its story makes clear that it is not a series of end time predictions. The book cannot be reduced to a neat end-time chart. To treat Revelation this way misses the fact that it tells a story that stretches all the way back to the first creation, and then stretches forward to the new creation. Also, much of Revelation develops as a cycle, where the author covers the same ground over and over, using different images. Furthermore, the sequence that we find in Revelation is the sequence in which John saw things ("I saw") not the sequence in which the events will take place, so that we can construct a detailed end-time scenario. So the careful reader will say, "Note to self: do not reduce Revelation to a chronological end-time chart of future events."

More importantly, the story of Revelation has much to say about who God is, and what he has accomplished and will accomplish through the Lamb, Jesus Christ. But the story has profound implication for what the church is to do, since the church is God's agent for carrying out his purposes on earth. In a nutshell, the church is to be a faithful witness. The church is to be part of God's story by fulfilling its faithful witness in the world. The church as the people of God is to witness to the reality of God and his kingdom, and to the Lamb who is faithful and true. The church is called upon to worship God and the Lamb, to join in heaven in acknowledging the sovereignty of God the creator, and the Lamb as the one worthy to bring God's redemptive plan to its completion. The church brings heaven down to earth when it joins in heaven in worship by acknowledging God as the sovereign creator of all things. When they do this, the Lord's prayer already begins to find fulfillment, with God's kingdom and will be accomplished on earth in the worshiping church, as it is in heaven. Until the day it comes in fullness, the church is to continue to pray the Lord's prayer: your kingdom come, your will be done on earth as it is in heaven.

The church is also to be a model of what life will be like in the new creation. As a kingdom of priests the church is to represent God's kingdom and presence here on earth. People should be able to look at the church, their faithful witness, their worship, and their unqualified obedience to God and the Lamb, and see a glimpse of life in the new creation in advance of its final and perfect establishment (21:1—22:5). This means that the church holds to a set of counter-values to those of the world, which brings them into direct conflict with the world and its values. Revelation makes it clear that there are two starkly different choices to follow: the way of God and the Lamb, or the way of the Dragon and the beasts. But the church is called upon to maintain this faithful witness to God and the Lamb to the very end, no matter what consequences it brings in a world that resists and opposes

God and his kingdom. Yet it is through the faithful witness of the church that the world will see the one true God and turn in repentance to "follow the Lamb wherever he goes" (14:4).

Key #5

BEASTS, AND BOWLS, BEACONS, AND BEELZEBUB

Mapping Metaphors in Revelation?

PROBABLY THE BIGGEST OBSTACLE for the modern-day reader in understanding Revelation is what to do with the images. And there are a lot of them! In almost every section of the book the reader is confronted with a *potpourri* of fantastic images: living creatures that are a combination of animal features, locusts with human heads and tails like scorpions, a lamb that was slain but still walking around with horns and eyes, a dragon that can spew out water and beasts with seven heads, fire mixed with hail, an abyss blowing smoke, talking eagles, and on and on. What are we to make of such strange phenomena? When I was first learning to read the book of Revelation, I was taught over and over again that the language of Revelation should be treated *literally*. The iron-clad rule that I heard regularly enforced was, "Interpret Revelation literally, unless there is a good reason not to." I learned that the correct response was that there was really no good reason not to! And so like many budding Revelation enthusiasts I tried to make sense of Revelation's images by interpreting them literally. After all, I was told, this is the word of God, and it demands that we treat it with the utmost seriousness. Who could argue with that? Furthermore, interpreting Revelation's images literally was the only way to avoid the subjectivity that would come if anyone tried to treat the images in any other way.

Maybe this is how you were taught to read Revelation as well. Literally! But is that the best way to read a book like Revelation? Or is there a better way? For a start, let me point you to two things that the careful reader should note that suggests that "literal" does not do justice to the book of Revelation. First, we saw in the first chapter of this book ("A Genre Like no Other: What kind of weird book is this anyway?") that Revelation belongs to an ancient type of writing that we call an "apocalypse." An apocalypse was a record of the author's visionary experience, and a key feature of this kind of writing was that it communicated symbolically, not literally. Therefore, as an apocalypse, a revelation from Jesus Christ to John, we should expect that it will communicate through symbols, not literally. To interpret Revelation symbolically (or better, metaphorically) is not some arbitrary move. I am not suggesting this just because we want to, or just because we don't know how to handle the strange images, so we decide to revert to symbolic inter-pretation. No. This is what the type of literature demands. As an apocalypse, Revelation requires that we read it symbolically, not literally.

Second, in one place Jesus himself interprets the images that John sees for John and his readers in John's inaugural vision in chapter 1. In this open-ing chapter of Revelation John sees a vision of the exalted, glorified Christ. He is described in terms of the Son of Man in Dan 7, and then John tells us that he was standing in the middle of seven lampstands (vv. 12–13) and that he was holding seven stars in his hand (v. 16). Jesus himself interprets these last two features for John: the seven stars are the seven angels of the churches, and the seven lampstands are the seven churches (see chs. 2–3). In other words, Jesus does not take the vision literally, but interprets these features symbolically; they represent or refer to something else: angels and churches! Someone might respond, "But we can only interpret this sym-bolically because Jesus does it here; but the places where Revelation is not interpreted we should assume it is literal!" But will this hold up?

It may also be helpful to notice how Jesus himself is described in Rev-elation. John has three main visions of Jesus Christ. The first one comes in the chapter we just looked at, 1:15–17.

Notice how Jesus is described: a son of man (from Dan 7), clothed with a long robe, wearing a golden belt, with eyes like flames of fire, and his feet like bronze, his voice like the sound of rushing waters, with a sword coming out of his mouth, and his appearance as the shining of the sun at full heat! Now notice the second vision in chapter 5. In this vision of Jesus John sees a Lamb who was slain, but who has seven horns and eyes (5:6). Compare this to the third vision of the Lord found in 19:11–16. Here Christ is depicted as a rider on a white horse, wearing a white road, with a tattoo on his thigh and a sword coming out of his mouth. What are we to make of these diverse pictures of Jesus? Are these literal descriptions of Jesus? Is this what Jesus will look like if we could take a photo of him? If so, is there more than one Jesus since they look so different? Or which version is correct? Maybe Jesus can transform himself or metamorphize into different shapes at will? I don't know of any well-meaning Christian who has ever answered "yes" to any of these questions. These are not literal pictures of Jesus, but different perspectives on who Jesus is that tell us something about his work and character through symbolism. They communicate that Jesus is a righteous judge (sword coming out of his mouth, rider on a white horse), that Jesus is the sacrificial lamb in fulfillment of the Old Testament (slain Lamb), that he is stable and powerful (bronze feet, horns), all-seeing and knowing (eyes of fire, seven eyes). John's visions are not literal descriptions of what Jesus looks like, but symbolic visions that say something in a powerful way of who Jesus is and what he does. So Revelation itself tells us that it is not meant to be taken literally.

WHAT IS A METAPHOR?

One of the things that distinguishes Revelation from all other books in the New Testament is the amount of symbolism in the book. In virtually every verse of Revelation the reader is met with symbolic language. But here we need to watch our language. It would be more accurate to say that Revelation is full of *metaphors*.[1] What is a *metaphor*? At a very basic level, metaphor is the use of language to shed light on one reality by referring to a totally different reality. Metaphors place side-by-side two words or concepts from very different parts of our world.[2] Another way of saying it is that metaphors are the use of language figuratively.[3] Words can have a literal meaning, but they can also have a figurative meaning. A metaphor is when a word is used outside of its normal or literal meaning, or used figuratively. For example, if I say "Peter is a snake" I have used one element, a reptile, to shed light on or say something about a completely different reality, a human being. This phrase is not meant to literally suggest Peter is a snake (unless I have a pet snake that I named Peter!), but it is meant to be taken figuratively or metaphorically. By placing side-by-side two elements that are different and don't normally belong to one another, a human being and a snake, I am able to shed light on the reality I am talking about, in this case what Peter is like. By saying Peter is a snake, I am using one feature of a snake—it is cunning, crafty, sneaky—to say something about Peter's character. I am not implying that Peter is slimy to the touch, or that he slithers around on the

1. Paul, *Revelation*, 16–17.
2. Paul, "Book of Revelation."
3. Sandy, *Plowshares and Pruning Hooks*, 73–74.

floor or ground. Rather, I am interested in what the term "snake" usually suggests when it is used of people: cunning, crafty, deceptive. Metaphors also have a powerful impact on us. I could say, "Peter is sneaky or deceptive; so you should be careful." But surely it is more powerful and effective to say, "Peter is a snake!" especially if I hate snakes (I do!) and recoil at the sight of one. That is, metaphors impact not only our minds but our emotions and get us to see things in a new light. If I say, "She threw me under the bus," I am not suggesting someone literally threw me under a bus moving at cruising speed out on the highway. It is a metaphorical or figurative expression that communicates the idea of "betraying someone for our own advantage, such as to avoid blame." Metaphors are a powerful means of communication.

SOME MAJOR METAPHORS IN REVELATION

Revelation is chock full of metaphors, or figurative use of language. We have already seen that Satan is referred to by the figure of a dragon. To use another example from above, by referring to Jesus Christ as a Lamb, two very different realities, a person and an animal, are placed side-by-side in order to shed light on that reality: Jesus suffers for his people and his death is a sacrifice for the sins of his people (in fulfillment of the Old Testament sacrificial lamb). Jesus is not literally a Lamb (an animal with hooves and who bleats), but metaphorically identifying Jesus with a Lamb says something about who Jesus is and what he has come to do. Or to take another example from above, when Jesus is described as having a sword coming out of his mouth, this is not a literal description of what Jesus looks like, but metaphorically says something about Jesus: he brings about judgment by speaking the word! This is what Jesus was doing when he interpreted the lampstands in 1:20. Lampstands were a literal piece of the furniture in the Old Testament tabernacle and temple, but here they have a figurative meaning. By placing two things beside each other that don't normally belong together, lampstands (a piece of furniture in the temple) and churches (made of people), he is speaking metaphorically, and saying something about the church's role in the world: they are to be faithful witnesses and represent God's presence in the world as his priests.

A key in understanding John's use of metaphor is that they must be understood in light of the historical context of the book. They must mean what John and his readers would have understood them to mean, and they would have referred to persons, places, and things in their own world.[4] In the same way that we are familiar with the images that we see in a political

4. Klein et al., *Biblical Interpretation*, 565.

cartoon, Uncle Sam, an eagle, a donkey and an elephant, the first readers would have been familiar with the metaphors John was using and would have associated them with realities in their own day. Our challenge is to figure out the meaning of the metaphors for the first readers in their context. When I was working for a rancher in Montana he one day asked me to help him dismantle an old cabin. Some of the logs were still good, and he wanted to use them to build his own cabin. When we started to remove the logs, I noticed newspaper stuffed in the cracks between the logs, probably to keep the cold Montana winter winds out. These papers dated from around the 1940s. One of the features that caught my eye was the political cartoons. But as I looked at them I could not make much sense of them. Upon reflection I discovered why. First, I was unfamiliar with the historical and political landscape of that time; second, I did not understand the meaning of some of the images in those cartoons. This is what the modern reader of Revelation is up against. We need to understand the meaning of the images in light of the historical context and what the first readers would have understood.

We have already noticed a number of times in this book the important role the dragon and beast play in Revelation's story. The beast is the means by which Satan, the dragon, carries out his deceptive and persecuting activity on earth (ch. 13). The beast comes up out of the abyss in 11:7, showing his demonic, evil nature (the abyss is the home of demons; see 9:1–3). Who is this beast? I once had a friend tell me in all seriousness that he could tell we were not in the end times because he had not yet seen any beasts or dragons walking around. He took the image of the beast very literally! But since Revelation communicates in metaphors, we should probably not expect to see a live dragon or beast parading around the globe. Instead, we need to ask what or who the beast refers to, and what the image of the beast is communicating. If you are a first-century Christian living in the shadow of the Roman Empire, with an emperor that opposed God and his people, who are you going to identify the beast with? Probably Rome and/or its emperor. John's imagery may be ambiguous here: does it refer to Rome, or the emperor, or perhaps both? The beast was a figure that suggested evil, chaos, anti-godly power—just how John wants his readers to see Rome and its emperor. The figure of a beast is used to reveal the true character of Rome, to expose its true colors.

Another example of how metaphors work in Revelation is the account of the two witnesses in Rev 11. Who are these two individuals, and what are they doing? Chapter 11 tells the story of two men who carry out their witness in the face of opposition and hostility. At first they appear to succeed, and can even breathe out fire to destroy those who try to destroy them. But then the beast (see above section) emerges and puts them to death. After a

brief period of time when the earth rejoices, God raises them up and vindicates them for all to see. Some would prefer to take this as a reference to
two literal individuals who will emerge in the end times and witness to the
world before the return of Christ. However, in the same way we understand
the beasts as metaphorical, this is how we should understand these two witnesses in Rev 11. They are metaphorical of the entire witnessing church, the
people of God. The fact that they are metaphorical for the entire church is
suggested by the fact that the two witnesses are identified as two lampstands
(v. 4). And we have already seen that Jesus himself identifies the lampstands
in 1:20 as the churches from chapters 2 to 3. Therefore, the two witnesses
metaphorically represent the church in its witness.

It might be similar to our reference to Uncle Sam in the United States
of America. When we refer to Uncle Sam, or see a picture of Uncle Sam, we
know that it is not referring to a literal individual, but to the United States
government, an institution made up of many people and parts. If we go to
the nation's capital, Washington, DC, we don't expect to see a literal Uncle
Sam walking around the streets of the city. We know that he is metaphorical
for the entire government. In a similar way, we should see the two witnesses
in Rev 11 not literally as referring to two specific people, but metaphorically
referring to the entire witnessing church. The fact that there are only two
is probably because in chapters 2 to 3 only two of the seven churches were
faithful witnesses and receive a positive evaluation from the risen Lord,
Smyrna (2:8–11) and Philadelphia (3:7–13). This story of the two witnesses,
then, charts a course for what the church, the people of God, are to be doing
on earth during the time when Rome (and any other empire) rules and until
Christ returns: they are to be God's faithful witnesses, even in the face of
opposition, and even death and apparent defeat at the hands of the world.

THE NUMBERS IN REVELATION

A special case of John's metaphors is the numbers found in Revelation.
Many readers might agree with much of what has been said so far. It is easy
to see how the image of the slaughtered Lamb with horns and seven eyes
should be taken metaphorically, and it is easy to see how the beast can be
taken metaphorically to refer to a godless empire and its ruler (for John
and his readers, Rome and its emperor). But what about the numbers that
occur throughout Revelation? Revelation is full of numbers: four, seven, ten,
(and multiples), twelve (and multiples), 666, 144,000. There are also several
numbers which refer to periods of time: three-and-one-half years, forty-
two months, twelve-hundred and sixty days, one-thousand years. Should

we take all these numbers literally? Are some of them symbolic, or meta-phorical? Do the time periods refer to literal periods of time? Should we add some of them up to determine specific durations of time?

I would recommend that the same principle we use to understand the above images of Lamb, dragon, beasts, lampstands, and the two witnesses should be applied to the numbers and time periods in Revelation as well: they are to be understood metaphorically or figuratively. That is, they refer to real things or periods of time, but they describe them metaphorically rather than literally. Below is a run-down and brief description of the major numbers in Revelation and what they mean.

Four

Four (4) is the number of the earth. So in heaven there are four living crea-tures, probably angelic beings, that worship God and the Lamb surrounding the throne (4:6–8; 5:8). They represent all of creation, which God intends will one day worship him alone. In 7:1 an angel restrains the four winds in the four corners of the earth. And in 20:8 Satan deceives nations from the four corners of the earth. Four, then, symbolizes the entire earth in Revelation.

Seven

This is probably the most well-known number in the book of Revelation. It has its roots in the seven days of creation in Gen 1–2. Seven is the number of perfection and completeness. John addresses seven churches in chapters 2 to 3. Although this refers to seven literal, historical churches that can be located on a map, they symbolize the complete and full church. Much of Revelation is structured around three sets of seven judgments: the seven seals (ch. 6), seven trumpets (chs. 8–9), and seven bowls (ch. 16). The point is not that there are only seven judgments in precisely that order. The num-ber seven suggests that these judgments represent the perfect and complete judgments of God. There are seven thunders, the content of which John is not allowed to write down (10:3–4). There are seven horns on the dragon (12:3) and the beast (13:1) pointing to the complete and seemingly invin-cible power of the dragon and beast. We also read of seven spirits of God (1:4; 4:5). This is most likely a reference to the Holy Spirit, especially since in the first mention it occurs with a reference to God and to the Son (1:4–6):

> Grace to you and peace from the one who was, and who is, and who is coming and from *the seven spirits which are before His throne*, and from Jesus Christ, the faithful witness, the firstborn from the dead, and the ruler of the kings of the earth.

The seven Sprits point to the perfect, complete, and full expression of the Spirit of God. Sometimes there is a sequence of seven that is not numbered. For example, there are seven beatitudes ("blessed") scattered throughout the book (1:3; 14:13; 16:15; 19:9; 20:6; 22:7, 14). This is probably not accidental, and the number seven indicates the perfect and full blessing of God on those who obey the book and persevere in obedience to God and the Lamb.

Ten

The number ten is a number of completeness or wholeness. It usually occurs in multiples, such as 1000 (see below), or 1000 multiplied with another number (e.g., 144,000). All of these indicate a large, full, and vast number.

Twelve

The number twelve is the number of the people of God. That is, wherever you see it in Revelation, it metaphorically refers to the church, God's true people. The number twelve is based on the twelve tribes of Israel and the twelve apostles of the Lamb. So the number twelve (and its multiples, 144) represents the people of God consisting of Jews, rooted in the Old Testament understanding of the people of God consisting of Jews, but also gentiles, who now with Jews make up the people of God, the church. The features and measurements of the new Jerusalem in Rev 21:9—22:5 are all twelve or multiples of twelve: twelve gates and twelve foundations (and stones); the length, width, and height are 12,000 stadia; the wall is 144 cubits thick; the tree of life yields twelve fruits each of the twelve months. That is, the measurements of the new Jerusalem are not literal architectural details that tell us the precise measurements of an end-time city, they tell us that the new Jerusalem is the home of, and is to be identified with, the full, complete consummated people of God (see below on 144,000).

666

As we already noticed earlier in chapter 1, the number 666 is probably related to Nero's name, and probably is also to be seen as falling short of the perfect number 777. It is a number that represents the true nature of Rome's character, godless and oppressive. The main thing is to resist identifying this number with any modern-day items (computer chips, or other technologies).

144,000

The number 144,000 first occurs in 7:4 (and see 14:1, 3). The number derives from a multiple of twelve, the number of the people of God (12x12=144). This number 144 is then multiplied by one-thousand, a number indicating fulness and great magnitude. 144,000 is not a literal number of people that you can add up on a calculator, but is metaphorical of the complete and vast people of God, in fulfillment of both Old Testament Israel and the New Testament church, consisting of Jew and gentile.

Time Periods

Three-and-one-half Years ("time, times and half a time")

Most of the references to a period of time come in chapters 11 to 12. The first occurrence of three-and-one-half-years, or "time, times, and half a time", occurs in 12:14. This time period comes from the book of Daniel (7:25; 12:7: "time, times, and half a time"). The number three-and-one-half can be seen as one half of seven, or an incomplete number that falls far short of the perfect number seven. It suggests a period of time that is intense, but will not last: it will be cut short. John is telling us that the period of tribulation anticipated by Daniel (7:25; 12:7) has already begun with the death and resurrection of Christ and will continue until Christ returns to cut it off. Though it is common to take this number as referring to a specific future period of time right before the coming of Christ, the number instead metaphorically refers to the entire period of time between the death and resurrection of Christ and his second coming at the end of history. That whole period of time is characterized as three-and-one-half years. So obviously, this does not refer to a literal period of time (two-thousand years later it is still going on!). Rather, it says something about the nature and character of the period of time of the church's existence between the first and second comings of Christ: it will be an intense period of persecution and struggle, but it will not last and will be cut short when Christ returns. Therefore, the designation three-and-one-half years refers to an actual period of time, the entire period between the first and second comings of Christ, a period of much longer than three-and-one-half years. But it does not describe that period of time literally, it is a metaphor that says something about the meaning and nature of the period of the church's existence between Christ's first and second comings. That is, it is not meant to tell us about the duration of that time, but the character of that time: it is a time of intense conflict and persecution, but it will not last and will be cut off.

John uses time periods metaphorically, or figuratively, elsewhere. In 17:12 the kings that serve the beast receive authority for "one hour." It is almost impossible to think of a scenario of all the kings ruling for a period of only sixty minutes![5] Just one chapter later (ch. 18) John describes Babylon's (Rome's) fall as taking place in one day (v. 8). But a few verses later it takes place in one hour (v. 19)! John is not giving us chronological details (otherwise there is a contradiction here). Instead, he is using time periods figuratively, here probably to refer to the quick and swift manner of Babylon's fall, perhaps to contrast with her claim to be eternal Rome.

We often use periods of time metaphorically. If someone interrupts our work, we may reply by saying, "Just a minute," while we finish up what we are doing. The time that that person had to wait may be much longer than a minute, or even shorter. But the purpose of this expression is not to designate a literal period of time, but to say something like, "Please wait, and your wait will not be very long." Or we might say something like, "That project would take me a thousand years to complete." The purpose is not to specify a literal period of a thousand years, especially since I would never live that long. Rather, this designation says something like, "This project would take an extraordinarily long time to complete, and I would probably never get it done." In a similar way, time periods in Revelation are important not for the temporal information they convey, but metaphorically for the meanings they convey about the period of the church's existence. John is not interested in calendars and clocks. The time periods don't tell us *how long*, but *what is the meaning*.

Forty-two Months

A little simple math reveals that forty-two months (11:2; 13:5) roughly equals three-and-one-half years. The period of forty-two months seems to be an alternative way of referring to the same period of time as the three-and-one-half years in Revelation: the entire period of the history of the

5. Koester, *Revelation and the End of All Things*, 108.

church between the first and second comings of Christ. But why a different number? Why forty-two months? The number forty plays a key role in the Old Testament and the life of the nation Israel. The number forty refers to the time of Israel's testing in the wilderness (Duet 8:2; Acts 13:18), and refers to the number of stages in the journey or places they camped on their journey through the desert (Num 33).[6] The forty-two months in Rev 11–13, then, recalls the period of testing of Israel in the wilderness and here refers to the period of time (between the first and second comings of Christ) as a period of testing and protection for the churches. Like the three-and-one-half years, the forty-two months refers to an actual period of time, but it does not describe it literally or tell us the duration of that period (again, that time has gone on for two-thousand years so far), but rather it indicates its character and meaning: it is a period of testing, but also protection.

1260 Days

Again, simple math will tell you that 1260 days is an alternative way of refer-ring to forty-two months and three-and-one-half years. It is used back-to-back with forty-two months in 11:2–3 and it is used to refer to the same event of the woman's flight to and preservation in the desert in 12:6, 14. It is not clear in Revelation why John uses the designation 1260 days. It is possible that it is John's variation (to fit three-and-one-half years and forty-two months) of Daniel's number 1290 (or 1335) days (12:11; see v. 12). But whatever the case, John uses this time designation to refer to the same pe-riod of time as the three-and-one-half years and the forty-two months: the entire period of the history of the church from the death and resurrection of Christ to his second coming at the end of history. Like the image of the three-and-one-half years and forty-two months, the reference to 1260 days probably also indicates a period of persecution that is intense but limited.

The following chart is meant to show how each of the time references refer to the same period of time: the entire period between the first and second comings of Christ. They are different ways of looking at the same time period; they are not meant to be added up.

---

6. Beale, *Revelation*, 565–67; Paul, *Revelation*, 197.

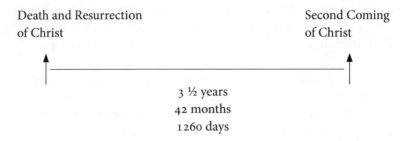

Death and Resurrection   Second Coming
of Christ   of Christ

3 ½ years
42 months
1260 days

There is no indication in Revelation at all that they are to be added up to arrive at a seven years of tribulation, or that they designate a sequence of time
periods that can be added up and allow us to construct an end-time chart.[7]
Instead, they serve to interpret the character of this age for the church: intense conflict, even persecution, but it won't last long and will be cut short
at the second coming of Christ. This period of time is a time of testing and
God's provision and protection. Also, by putting a number on it this period
of time, John gives a sense of order and control. This period of time is not
out of control but has a divine purpose and is under God's control. The
people of God in the first century, or any century, where it finds itself in
a life and death struggle with the powers of this world, can take comfort
from the message of these numbers: God is in control, things are moving
towards a goal, and God has a purpose for what the people of God are going
through. That is the message of three-and-one-half years, forty-two months,
and 1260 days.

One-Thousand Years

The period of one-thousand years occurs only in Rev 20:2–6:

> And he seized the dragon, the serpent of old, who is the devil
> and Satan, and he bound him for a *thousand years*. And he threw
> him into the abyss and locked and sealed it over him in order
> that he might not deceive the nations any longer until the *thou-
> sand years* are completed. And I saw thrones, and those seated
> upon them, and judgment was given for them, and [I saw] the
> souls of those who had been beheaded because of the witness of
> Jesus and the word of God, and those who did not worship the
> beast or is image and did not receive his mark upon their fore-
> heads and upon their hands, and they lived and reigned with

---

7. Koester, *Revelation and the End of All Things,* 108. Koester notes that if you added
up all the references to 3 ½ years, 42 months, and 1,260 days in Rev 11–13, you would
end up with way more than 7 years!

Christ for a *thousand years*. The rest of the dead did not live until after the *thousand years*. This is the first resurrection. Blessed and holy is the one who participates in the first resurrection; the second death will not have authority over them, but they will be priests of God and of Christ and they will reign with him for a *thousand years*.

This passage and the one-thousand-year period of time has become associated with the doctrine of the Millennium, the thousand-year reign of Christ. There has been much debate throughout church history and among Christians and denominations on what this period of time refers to. Some take it more or less literally as referring to an exact period of one-thousand years that will occur in the future, when Christ and his people will reign on earth (premillennialism). Others take it as symbolically, or metaphorically, referring to the entire period of time between the first and second comings of Christ (amillennialism). Most likely, we should take the reference to the thousand years in the same way we take the other numbers in Revelation, metaphorically. That is, it is not designating a literal period of time, but is more interested in saying something about the meaning of that time. In Rev 20:4–6 the one-thousand refers to the resurrection and vindication of the people of God. It is metaphorical for the complete vindication of the people of God at their resurrection at the second coming of Christ, but does not refer to a period of duration at all. The reference to the one-thousand years occurs within the context of Satan's judgment. While Satan is now judged, those he harmed and put to death are raised and vindicated: they now reign with Christ. The guilty party, Satan, is now accused and condemned, and those he falsely accused and put to death are raised and vindicated. This is what is symbolized by the one-thousand years. The one-thousand years is meant to contrast with the periods of time that referred to their life here on earth, a life of persecution and conflict: three-and-one-half years, forty-two months, 1260 days. Now their vindication is far, far greater- one-thousand years! The message of the millennium is that the vindication of the people of God at their resurrection in the future will far exceed and compensate for anything they suffered here on earth at the hands of the Enemy![8]

Colors

John even uses colors symbolically in his book.[9] For example, gold indicates purity, beauty, and God's presence. The new Jerusalem and its streets are

8. Mathewson, *Companion to the Book of Revelation*, 110–14.

9. Gorman, *Reading Revelation Responsibly*, 17–18.

made of gold; it is a place of purity and of God's presence with his people (21:18, 21). Black symbolizes death and destruction. The third horse in 6:5 is black, fitting for a plague of destruction. White is the color that signifies conquering, victory, and purity. Therefore, the saints are given white robes, indicating the fact that they have overcome, and that they are pure (6:11; 7:9, 13–14). It is the color of Christ's horse in 19:11. Red indicates blood and violence, so it is a fitting color for the second horse (6:4), which brings slaughter, and the dragon (12:3), who puts the saints to death.

WHERE DOES JOHN GET HIS METAPHORS?

John uses metaphors that his readers would have been familiar with, that would have made sense to them. The primary background for John's metaphors is the Old Testament, the Scriptures of the church in the first century. Beginning with the very first chapter, nearly every verse in the book of Revelation resonates with the Old Testament. But John does not signal the presence of the Old Testament in his book in the way some other New Testament writers sometimes do. For example, he does not introduce references to the Old Testament with something like, "This took place to fulfill what was spoken in the prophet Isaiah" or "Just as it is written." You find this way of referring to the Old Testament especially in the first two chapters of Matthew. The birth of Jesus and all the major events in his early childhood are explained with a quote from the Old Testament, introduced with a clear signal that basically says, "Here comes an Old Testament quote." Therefore, when Joseph and Mary take Jesus down to Egypt to escape the death threats of Herod, Matthew quotes an Old Testament passage from Hos 11:1: "And so it was fulfilled what had been spoken by the Lord through the prophet, 'Out of Egypt I have called my son.'"

However, a quick glance through Revelation's pages reveals a lack of any clear "signals" that the Old Testament is being quoted. There are no "This took place to fulfill what was spoken by the prophet." Instead, John simply weaves the words of the Old Testament into the record of his vision without telling you. But this would not escape the notice of readers who were familiar with the Old Testament (such as John's first readers). Readers with minds saturated with the Old Testament could not help but pick up on John's use of the Old Testament, even without an introduction to signal it.

The Vision of Christ in 1:12–15

For example, John begins his book with a description of a vision of the risen Christ in 1:12–15 (see above) in dazzling splendor and attire.

> 12 I turned around to see the voice that was speaking to me. And when I turned I saw seven golden lampstands, 13 and among the lampstands was someone like a son of man, dressed in a robe reaching down to his feet and with a golden sash around his chest. 14 The hair on his head was white like wool, as white as snow, and his eyes were like blazing fire. 15 His feet were like bronze glowing in a furnace, and his voice was like the sound of rushing waters. 16 In his right hand he held seven stars, and coming out of his mouth was a sharp, double-edged sword. His face was like the sun shining in all its brilliance.

The vision is stunning and breathtaking. This picture that the author gives of Christ is a compilation of images from an array of Old Testament passages. The image of the seven lampstands in v. 12 comes from the lampstands in the tabernacle and temple (Exod 25:31–40). When John describes Christ as "someone like a son of man" (v. 13) he is drawing on Dan 7:13, where Daniel has a vision of one like a son of man. John's description of Jesus' attire as consisting of a robe reaching down to his feet (v. 13) belongs to the wardrobe of the high priest Aaron (Exod 28:4; Zech 3:4). The portrait of his hair on his head as white as snow as wool (v. 14) derives from Daniel's description of the Ancient of Days in 7:9. Jesus's facial feature of eyes like flames of fire and his feet like glowing bronze (vv. 14–15) come from Daniel (10:5–6). His voice sounding like rushing water comes right out of Ezek 1:24. The double-edged sword that Christ wields (v. 16) John finds in Isa 49:2, while the description of his face as shining like the sun probably reflects Moses on mount Sinai.[10]

So you can see that every major feature of this portrait of the risen Christ comes right out of the Old Testament, though John never tells you that explicitly. He just assumes that his readers, familiar with the Old Testament, will see the connections. Furthermore, when John makes a reference to an Old Testament text it is usually just the tip of the iceberg of the context of the passage that he refers to. Icebergs on the sea only reveal part of their entire mass. Most of it lies beneath the surface of the ocean, with just a small portion sticking out. The same is true of many of John's references to the Old Testament. The verse that John actually alludes to is just the tip of the iceberg, with the broader context of that Old Testament reference

---

10. Paul, *Revelation*, 73.

lying just beneath the surface. That is, his Old Testament references usually bring with them their meaning from their original contexts. In Dan 7 the son of man is an exalted, heavenly figure who receives a kingdom. In the above portrait of the risen Christ, the robe that reaches to his feet is more than just an interesting piece of clothing but comes from the description of the highpriest in the Old Testament, and points to Jesus as priest, who tends to the lampstands, the churches, which are God's temple. The sword coming out of his mouth suggests that Jesus is also judge, and that is what he does in chapters 2 to 3: he judges or evaluates his churches by his word. Several images from the Old Testament in their original context applied to God—the sword coming out of his mouth, his voice as rushing waters, the hair on head as white as wool (the Ancient of Days in Dan 7). Jesus shares in the very identity and being of God. John equates Jesus with God, so that later in 5:12 Jesus, the Lamb, and God share the same throne and receive the exact same worship. When the reader identifies the Old Testament reference in John's depiction of Jesus in 1:12–16, new meanings emerge that would not be discovered apart from the OT context.

The Seals, Trumpets, and Bowls

Another example of how the Old Testament background influences our understanding of John's vision is the trumpet and bowl judgment sequences in chapters 8 to 9 and 16. Though the sequence is a little different in both sets of plague-judgments, there are similarities in the judgments.

Trumpets	Bowls
#1 hail, fire, blood	#1 ugly and painful sores
#2 sea turned to blood	#2 sea turned to blood
#3 waters are embittered	#3 rivers become blood
#4 darkness	#4 intense heat from sun
#5 locusts from the abyss	#5 darkness
#6 four angels and a large army	#6 evil spirits as frogs
#7 God's kingdom comes (11:15–19)	#7 great earthquake

A quick glance at these two lists of judgments reveals similarities between trumpets 1, 2 and bowls 1, 2, and between trumpet 4 and bowl 5 especially. This may point to the fact that there is some overlap in these judgments and when they take place. But a more important feature is seen when the two lists are added together. When you read of water turned to blood, darkness covering the earth, sores, locusts, and frogs, what comes to your mind? Some of you may have noticed the parallels between these plagues and another famous set of plagues: the Exodus (Exod 7–11).[11] In the book of Exodus, God poured out plagues on Egypt, who was enslaving and oppressing God's covenant people. Parallel to the trumpets and bowls, the Exodus plagues consisted of water turning to blood, hail, frogs, sores, darkness, and death. In fact, the response to the plagues in Revelation, refusal to repent (9:20–21; 16:11), mirrors Pharoah's response to the Exodus plagues where he hardened his heart (Exod 7:22; 8:15, 19, 32; 9:7, 12, 35; 10:20, 27).

John's point, then, does not appear to be to predict a series of seven, literal plagues that will occur in this exact order, as much as we might wish he had. Rather, his main point is that we draw the connection with the original Exodus plagues. The central message of Rev 8–9, 16 is that in the same way that God judged a godless, idolatrous nation in the past (Egypt), so he will do it again. John's purpose is not a literal description of what the judgments will look like (remember, Revelation is metaphorical), rather it is to reveal the meaning and certainty of God's judgment. It is probably impossible for modern readers to know exactly what these judgments are or will look like, and John may not have intended to give such information. Rather, the key is for the reader to recognize the Exodus connection, which tells us something about the meaning and purpose of God's judgment. This may seem less exciting for the modern-day reader or preacher, but it is more accurate to the kind of literature Revelation is, and the Old Testament Exodus background to the trumpets and bowls.

The Prostitute-Babylon

In Rev 17 we are introduced to the city Babylon, which is also described as a prostitute. The image of Babylon also has a storied Old Testament background. Babylon was an idolatrous, ungodly, economically unjust world power which oppressed God's people, taking them into exile. The Old Testament prophets predict the historical city's destruction by God's judgment (Isa 13:19–22; Jer 50–51). Babylon is used by John now as a metaphor for Rome, because the same idolatrous, godless, oppressive, arrogant system found in Babylon is now resident in Rome. John is not predicting the rise of Babylon again but is using Babylon as a metaphor to uncover the true nature of the Roman Empire in his day. Even the image of a prostitute carries Old Testament background, where it referred to unclean, ungodly empires that seduced other nations into participating in their unjust economic practices

11. See deSilva, *Discovering Revelation*, 116.

(Isa 23:7, 15–18; Ezek 16:1–36; Hos 4:11–12).[12] Now Rome is doing the same thing. She is seducing other peoples and nations to be involved in her idolatrous and unjust practices. And at least one church in Rev 3:14–22 is guilty of becoming wealthy off its association with Rome: Laodicea!

Therefore, when making sense of Revelation's images, look for the Old Testament. Read the Old Testament, then hold it up as a mirror to Revelation to see where it is reflected. Here the reader will find two kinds of tools helpful for identifying Old Testament references in Revelation. First, we must rely on good commentaries (see ch. 1 above). They will usually discuss the most important Old Testament references in Revelation. Second, most good English translations and study Bibles will alert you to Old Testament references in marginal notes or footnotes. It is important to go back and read these Old Testament passages in their original context. The next step is to see what meaning it adds to Revelation, what difference the Old Testament reference makes in reading the passage. What would you miss without a knowledge of the Old Testament background? It is safe to say that without an understanding of the Old Testament the book of Revelation will not unlock its full treasures to the reader.

THE POWER OF REVELATION'S METAPHORS

Words are powerful things. With them we can cheer someone up, or tear someone down. Metaphors are even more powerful. They have the ability to evoke a response in a way that more straightforward speech does not. They arrest our attention, affect our minds and our emotions, get us to see things in a way that we never have before. Metaphors are powerful in another way, too. They have the power to reach beyond their immediate application to further applications. That is, metaphors transcend time. They have the ability to have multiple references beyond just their original usage by an author. A good example is the image of the beast in chapter 13. We saw in an earlier chapter that the beast was a metaphor that most likely referred to the Roman Empire/the emperor in the first century. This is what the readers probably would have identified the first beast as. The image of a beast evoked notions of evil, chaos, the demonic. But what is interesting is that the beast from chapter 13 is found at the final battle at the end of history, at the second coming of Christ, where he is defeated and thrown into the lake of fire (19:20). So how does the beast which inspires first-century Rome and its emperor still exist at the second coming of Christ? Metaphors have the

---

12. Beale, *Revelation*, 849–50.

power to transcend time. They often communicate archetypal realities that can extend beyond the original circumstances to which they are applied.

For example, the image of a beast has a history that predates John's use of it in Rev 13 to refer to the Roman Empire/emperor. A beast or dragon-like figure was used in the Old Testament to refer to godless, violent, oppressive empires of the past (Ps 73:13–14; Isa 27:1; 51:9; Ezek 29:3; Dan 7:1–7). John now sees that same godless, violent, oppressive power resident in the Roman Empire. And that same power will continue until Jesus returns at his second coming to bring it to an end. In this way, the same beastly power that inspired Rome can continue to inspire other kingdoms, nations, and empires. That does not mean that John predicted these, or that he saw other nations or countries beyond Rome. It means that John understood that the evil, godless, oppressive power of the beast that was at work in past empires was at work in Rome and would continue until Christ returned to judge and destroy it, whether that is Rome or some other empire (we know it is the latter, because we are two-thousand years down the road!). And we will never know exactly what form it will take just before Christ comes back to bring it to an end. For John, it could have ended with Rome, but John was not predicting that Christ would come back when Rome fell. He was only predicting that the beastly power behind Rome would eventually be destroyed in judgment at Christ's return. So metaphors have the ability to extend beyond their original references (Rome) to refer to similar situations and entities (other nations, empires, kingdoms) without suggesting John actually saw them or predicted their rise (the Nazi Regime, and whatever form the beast will take when Christ returns). Metaphors penetrate to the underlying theological meaning and the essential character of things that lies behind what they refer to.[13] The image of a beast, then, has the ability to penetrate beyond the Roman Empire to its true character and essential nature, a nature and character which can extend to other nations and empires until Christ returns to judge it.

The same can be said for the symbolism of Babylon in chapters 17 to 18. It is hard to think that the first readers would not have identified Babylon with Rome, especially since it is described as the city on seven hills (17:9), a well-known first-century label for Rome. The account of its destruction did have a fulfillment a couple hundred years after Revelation was written. But it appears to have a further fulfillment in the final judgment. Once again, John is using an image that has a history going all the way back to the Old Testament. That is, he is using an image that is not restricted to one period of time. As a metaphor, the image of Babylon penetrates to the

---

13. Bauckham, *Theology of Revelation*, 156. See Paul, *Revelation*, 30–34.

main theological meaning and essential character of Rome: it is godless, idolatrous, oppressive, murderous. But as a metaphor, its ability to uncover the true character of Rome has the ability to extend beyond first-century Rome to apply to other nations, empires, and kingdoms that would reflect that same character. You have heard the phrase, "if the shoe fits wear it." Something similar can be said of John's use of Babylon or the beast as a metaphor: if the prophetic shoe fits, wear it![14] Whatever nation chooses to act like Rome, there is the power of the beast and Babylon.

John's metaphors have the ability to penetrate to the essential meaning and character of the events they refer to in the first century. This gives them the power to move beyond the first-century events and extend all the way to the second coming of Christ because they focus on the essential meaning and character that lies behind first century persons and events. In this way, John's visions have direct relevance to the first century, but also transcends its original context and has relevance to later situations, until Christ returns. This does not mean that John predicted modern day nations and empires, but that he understood that the beast and his power would only be vanquished at the second coming of Christ. And this is what gives John's images the power to find further applications until Christ returns.

PUTTING IT INTO PRACTICE

We have already looked at several passages from Revelation to demonstrate how John uses metaphors to communicate to his readers then and now. I want to consider one more example of how John uses a metaphor and how it impacts interpreting a part of his vision in light of how metaphors work and in light of its Old Testament background. The passage is Rev 21:1—22:5, and the metaphor is "the temple." In 21:1—22:5, at the climax of his vision, John sees the culmination of God's redemptive purposes in a vision of a new creation, and a new Jerusalem, with God and the Lamb dwelling in their midst. In 21:3 John, quoting the Old Testament from Ezek 37:36–37, says that God's tabernacle dwelling will be with his people: "Behold, the tabernacle dwelling of God is with humanity, and he will dwell with them, and they will be his people, and he will be God himself with them." So the reader might expect to find a tabernacle or temple described somewhere in 21:1—22:5. The reader's expectation of this is heightened when he or she gets to 21:18–21 and the description of twelve stones, which correspond

---

14. Richard Bauckham uses a different saying, "if the cap fits, wear it" and concludes that "Any society whom Babylon's cap fits must wear it" (*Theology of Revelation*, 156; see also 153).

to the twelve stones on the breastplate of the highpriest (Exod 28:17–20; 39:8–14). But the reader's expectation is shattered when he or she gets to 21:21: "And I did not see a temple in it." So God is going to establish his tabernacle-dwelling among his people just like he promised in Ezek 37 but without a temple! What is even more intriguing is that the Old Testament passage that has one of the great influences on John's vision of 21:1—22:5 is Ezek 40–48; and at the very center of Ezekiel's vision is a rebuilt *temple*. Ezekiel spends seven chapters describing the rebuilt temple! But now John does not see one! But I would suggest that just because John does not see a separate, physical temple in the new Jerusalem, does not mean that there is not one. John makes it pretty clear that the temple of the Old Testament now metaphorically refers to God and the Lamb's dwelling with their people directly: "God and the Lamb are its temple" (21:21).[15] But the temple has also become a metaphor for the people of God themselves. The people are now God's true temple where God dwells (21:3). When John describes the measuring of the new Jerusalem/people in 21:15–17, he is relying on Ezek 40–48. Only, John does not measure the temple; he measures the *new Jerusalem,* which is metaphorical of the people of God. So John applies Ezekiel's temple measuring to measuring the new Jerusalem. To support this, the layout of the city as a square in 21:16 ("the city was laid out like a square") resembles the layout of the temple in Ezek 48:35, and the very shape of the new Jerusalem as a cube (21:16: "its length, and width, and height were equal") resembles the shape of the holy of holies in the Old Testament temple (1 Kgs 6:20).[16] Even the stones from the breastplate of the highpriest (from Exod 28) are metaphorically equated with people: the Apostles of the Lamb (21:14).

There is a further step in John's equation. John tells us that the new Jerusalem is the bride of the Lamb, that is, the church, the people of God (21:9–10). The new Jerusalem is also a metaphor for the people of God. And that means that the temple in Ezekiel's vision and even in the original temple construction in Exodus, is now metaphorically applied to the people of God. Adding this all up, God's *people* are the new temple, the very place where God's presence dwells in fulfillment of Ezekiel's prophecy of a re-stored temple. Ezekiel's temple in 40–48 becomes a metaphor for the very people of God themselves as the true dwelling place of God. What Ezekiel's temple looked forward to has now been fulfilled, not in a physical structure, but in the people of God as God's dwelling place.

15. Robinson, *Temple of Presence.*
16. See Paul, *Revelation,* 350–51.

This is consistent with what we find elsewhere in the New Testament, where the people of God are frequently referred to with the metaphor of the temple (1 Cor 3:16; Eph 2:21–22; 1 Pet 2:5). God's people are the true temple where God dwells. The temple in the Old Testament has been transformed into a metaphor that now refers to the people themselves as the true temple of God. In Rev 21:1—22:5, now that all sin has been removed (chs. 19–20) and a new creation is established (21:1), there is no longer a need for a separate physical temple to mediate God's presence to his people. He can dwell directly in their midst. Therefore, they are now the true temple of God! One could say, while the other New Testament passages look at the incomplete temple under construction ("it is being built up"; Eph 2:22; 1 Pet 2:5), Rev 21:1—22:5 sees the completed temple in the new creation.

The image of the temple resonates with notions of God's presence, worship, holiness, and purity. As such, the vision of the completed temple in 21:1—22:5 is a call for the people of God to be God's temple in the present (see the image of lampstands in ch. 1). They are to reflect and represent God's presence to the rest of the world. They are to offer praise and worship, to sing the praises of God and the Lamb who have redeemed them. They are to live lives of purity and holiness in an ungodly world. The church as the temple is the witness (as lampstands) to the reality of God's presence in the world, and an anticipation of his unmediated presence in the new creation at the consummation of God's redemptive plan.[17]

---

17. For a detailed discussion of the theme of the temple in the New Testament and how it relates to the church's mission, see Beale, *Temple and the Church's Mission*.

TYING IT ALL TOGETHER
Let's Read the Book!

WE HAVE COVERED A lot of territory in this book. The road through Revelation has taken different twists and turns. To get back to our original metaphor, this book has attempted to provide you, the reader, with the keys to unlocking the treasures in the book of Revelation. One of the responses that I hear more than any other from readers of Revelation is that "I have always been afraid of this book." Hopefully, the exploration of the main keys for unlocking the treasures of Revelation has taken much of the fear out of reading this book. It was not meant to be a mysterious or frightening book, but a Revelation from God and Jesus Christ that offers a blessing for the one who hears/reads it and puts it into practice (1:3). In summary, what are the keys that you should hold firmly in your hand as you seek to open up this unique book of Revelation?

The first key to opening up the book of Revelation was to consider the unique literary genre of this book. It is actually a combination of three literary types: apocalypse, prophecy, and letter. Most misunderstandings of Revelation begin by failing to grasp the kind of book that it is. In other words, readers try to use a key that will not fit. And the main difficulty is—we don't really have anything like it today! An understanding of the type of book Revelation is will not solve all the problems, but it will help us to get off on the right foot to start with. All three kinds of literature represented in Revelation would have been familiar to the first readers; they would have known what they were listening to when it was read. As an apocalypse Revelation is an unveiling—it unveils the true nature of the world, and the true nature of what the first readers were going through. It provides its readers with a new perspective on the world and on their present day. Furthermore, it is important to recognize that as an apocalypse Revelation swims in the language of symbolism or metaphor. While it describes actual, real events in the author and readers' day and in the future, it describes them symbolically, or metaphorically, not literally. As a prophecy, Revelation is not primarily a prediction of the future, but is a message for the time of the readers. It both warns and encourages. So that is how we need to read it, not as a detailed road map of the future, but as a warning and encouragement to the people of God. As a letter, like any of Paul's letters in the New Testament, Revelation is addressing the specific needs and problems facing the seven churches in chapters 2 to 3. It would have made sense to them and addressed their needs. Any interpretation that John could not have intended and his first readers would never have understood is probably incorrect. This is the first key that allows us to open up the book of Revelation and get it to reveal its treasures. This key, recognizing the kind of literature Revelation is, explains the remaining keys on your key chain.

The second key to unlocking the treasures of the apocalypse is that Revelation must be understood in light of its original historical and cultural background. Revelation was addressing seven historical churches that found themselves immersed in Roman rule and culture. They were faced with the claims of Rome to be eternal, to bring peace, to offer salvation and economic prosperity. They lived in a culture surrounded by temples and altars to pagan gods, and even to the emperor. Christians were faced with pressures to conform or to face the consequences. This pressure came from outside the church, such as officials within the cities, or the Jewish synagogue. But some of the pressure came from within the church, from groups or individuals who encouraged compromise. To fail to participate would be a sign of ingratitude and would cause them to be looked at with suspicion or as poor citizens. Christians were faced with competing allegiances: God and the Lamb, or Caesar! Two of the churches refused to compromise their faithful witness to Jesus Christ in this environment, and they suffered the consequences—poverty, shunning, marginalization, and verbal assaults. But the other five churches had become complacent in their lives in their cities, or they compromised their faithful witness to Jesus Christ and the gospel by participating in the Roman economy and worship of the gods and the emperor. For the two churches that were suffering the consequences for maintaining their faithful witness, Revelation would serve as an encouragement and would provide staying power in the face of a difficult situation. But for the other five churches, Revelation would serve as a prophetic warning. It would call them to repent of their complacency and their compromise and would call them to faithful witness, no matter what the consequences as the hands of the Roman government. So a crucial key to unlocking the message of Revelation is to understand it in light of the historical context that it was addressing.

A third key to unlocking the treasures of the book of Revelation is to understand its main purposes. What was God trying to communicate through his prophet John? Here is where many readers go astray. Revelation was not meant to be a detailed prediction of the future. It was not as if John was looking into a crystal ball and seeing the future, centuries down the road from his own day. This would do little good for the first readers in chapters 2 to 3 if all John was doing was predicting a bunch of events that were going to happen centuries down the road from their own, events which they could not understand anyway. Instead, Revelation was written to be understood by the first readers and to address their needs and problems. John writes to inspire hope in God's people and to encourage faithful witness to Jesus in his churches. He writes to move them to a life of obedience to Jesus Christ. He writes to inspire worship of God and the Lamb by the people of God. He writes to shock his readers out of their complacency and compromise. He writes to unveil the bankruptcy of the Roman Empire and show its true colors: godlessness, idolatry, oppression, violence. Overall, John's main purpose is to inspire faithful witness through obedience and worship in the people of God, no matter what the consequences they might have to face. For any interpretation of Revelation to be valid, it must start from this overall purpose.

A fourth key for unlocking the riches of Revelation is to grasp its story. Revelation is not a collection of future predictions. It tells a story, a story with characters, good and evil, with a plot, tension, and a resolution. It is a story of how God and the Lamb establish their will and rule, rightly recognized in heaven, upon the earth. God's will is contested on earth by the dragon, Satan, the primary antagonist who works through two beasts and earthy rulers and empires to accomplish his nefarious purposes. Revelation is the story of how God through the Lamb, and through his people, his faithful witnesses, defeats the powers of evil and establishes his will and rule on earth, the new creation in 21:1—22:5. The seven churches in the first century Roman Empire are to see their specific stories against the backdrop of this larger story. Revelation is about how this larger story is being "acted out" in the specific lives of the seven churches in chapters 2 to 3. By seeing how the seven churches were part of this larger story, the church today can also find its place in the larger story of what God is doing, and what it means to be his faithful witnesses in a world that contests God's will and rule. When reading any section of Revelation, the reader must place it within the larger story that the book tells.

The fifth and final key that we discussed to unlocking the riches of the book of Revelation is coming to grips with its symbolism, or metaphors. While Revelation refers to real persons, places, and events, in John's day and in the future when Christ returns, it does not describe them literally but through metaphors. One of the most characteristic features of the book of Revelation is the metaphors that crowd its pages. The rule that "Revelation should be interpreted literally unless there is clear evidence not to" should be overturned and replaced with "Revelation should be interpreted symbolically unless there is good reason not to." This is not something we are arbitrarily advocating because we don't know what to do with this book. It is demanded by the very type of literature that Revelation is (an apocalypse), how Jesus himself interprets the images in 1:20, and just by the way Revelation uses language (notice how Christ is portrayed throughout the book). Metaphors have the power to impact not only our minds, but our hearts and emotions. They can communicate in ways that more straightforward or literal language cannot. To take Revelation symbolically is not to take it less seriously as God's word, but to take it more seriously, because that is the way that God has chosen to communicate through this unique book. The source for most of Revelation's images and metaphors is the Old Testament. John borrows the language of Old Testament prophets and even historical books to communicate his own vision. Often, these images carry with them the meaning they had and the broader context of their original context. In order to unlock the meaning of John's symbolism, the modern-day reader must have a good handle on the Old Testament. The Old Testament is like a mirror, that when you hold it up next to the book of Revelation you will find it reflected in virtually every page of Revelation.

So, armed with these keys to unlocking the message of Revelation, you are now ready to read the book. Hopefully, these keys can provide a more meaningful experience in reading the book of Revelation as God's word to his people. Hopefully it can remove some of the fear that plagues so many when they come to this New Testament book. Hopefully it will give you greater confidence in interpreting it and especially in applying it for today. And don't forget the many helpful teachers that are there to help you (see the commentaries listed in ch. 1). Now, go read Revelation!

BIBLIOGRAPHY

Ascough, Richard S. "Greco-Roman Religions and the Context of the Book of Revelation." In *The Oxford Handbook of the Book of Revelation*, 169–83. Edited by Craig R. Koester. Oxford: Oxford University Press, 2020.

Bauckham, Richard J. *Theology of the Book of Revelation*. Cambridge: Cambridge University Press, 1993.

Beale, Gregory K. *The Book of Revelation*. New International Greek Testament Commentary. Grand Rapids: Eerdmans, 1999.

———. *The Temple and the Church's Mission*. New Studies in Biblical Theology. Downers Grove, IL: InterVarsity, 2004.

Culy, Martin M. *The Book of Revelation: The Rest of the Story*. Eugene, OR: Pickwick, 2017.

deSilva, David A. *Discovering Revelation: Content, Interpretation, Reception*. London: SPCK, 2021.

———. *Unholy Allegiances: Heeding Revelation's Warning*. Peabody, MA: Hendrickson, 2013.

Fee, Gordon D., and Douglas Stuart. *How to Read the Bible for All Its Worth*. 3rd ed. Grand Rapids: Zondervan, 2003.

Gorman, Michael J. *Reading Revelation Responsibly: Uncivil Worship and Witness: Following the Lamb into the New Creation*. Eugene, OR: Cascade: 2011.

Klein, William W., et al. *Introduction to Biblical Interpretation*. 3rd ed. Grand Rapids: 2017.

Koester, Craig R. *Revelation and the End of All Things*. 2nd ed. Grand Rapids: Eerdmans, 2001.

Kraybill, J. Nelson. *Apocalypse and Allegiance: Worship, Politics, and Devotion in the Book of Revelation*. Grand Rapids: Brazos, 2010.

Mathewson, David L. *A Companion to the Book of Revelation*. Cascade Companions. Eugene, OR: Cascade, 2020.

———. "Social Justice in the Book of Revelation: Reading Revelation from Above." In *The Bible and Social Justice: Old Testament and New Testament Foundations for the Church's Urgent Call*, 176–97. McMaster New Testament Studies. Eugene, OR: Pickwick, 2015.

———. *Where is the Promise of His Coming? The Delay of the Parousia in the New Testament*. Eugene, OR: Cascade, 2018.

Paul, Ian. "The Book of Revelation: Image, Symbol and Metaphor." In *Studies in the Book of Revelation,* 131–47. Edited by Steve Moyise. Edinburgh: T. & T. Clark, 2001.

———. *Revelation.* Tyndale New Testament Commentaries. Downers Grove, IL: IVP Academic, 2018.

Resseguie, James L. *The Revelation of John: A Narrative Commentary.* Grand Rapids: Baker Academic, 2009.

Robinson, Andrea L. *Temple of Presence: The Christological Fulfillment of Ezekiel 40–48 in Revelation 21:1–22:5.* Eugene, OR: Wipf & Stock, 2019.

Sandy, Brent D. *Plowshares and Pruning Hooks: Rethinking the Language of Biblical Prophecy and Apocalyptic.* Downers Grove, IL: InterVarsity, 2002.

Schüssler Fiorenza, Elisabeth. *Revelation: Vision of a Just World.* Proclamation Commentaries. Minneapolis: Fortress, 1991.

Wainwright, Arthur W. *Mysterious Apocalypse: Interpreting the Book of Revelation.* Nashville: Abingdon, 1993.

Weima, Jeffrey A. D. *The Sermons to the Seven Churches of Revelation: A Commentary and Guide.* Grand Rapids: Baker, 2021.

Wilson, Mark W. *Biblical Turkey: A Guide to the Jewish and Christian Sites of Asia Minor.* 4th ed. Ege: Yayinlari, 2020.

AUTHOR INDEX

SUBJECT INDEX

SCRIPTURE INDEX